JEAN MONNET AND CANADA:
EARLY TRAVELS AND THE IDEA OF
EUROPEAN UNITY

European Union Studies

European Union Studies features the latest research on topics in European integration in the widest sense, including Europe's role as a regional and international actor. This interdisciplinary series publishes the research of Canadian and international scholars and aims at attracting scholars working in various disciplines such as economics, history, law, political science, and sociology. The series is made possible in part by a generous grant from the European Commission.

The first series of its kind in Canada, and one of only a few in North America, *European Union Studies* is unique in looking at the EU 'from the outside,' making sense not only of European integration but also of the role of the European Union as an international actor.

GENERAL EDITORS:

Jeffrey Kopstein
Professor of Political Science
Director, Centre for European, Russian, and Eurasian
    Studies
University of Toronto

Amy Verdun
Professor of Political Science
Director, Jean Monnet Centre of Excellence
University of Victoria

For a list of books published in the series, see page 110.

TRYGVE UGLAND

Jean Monnet and Canada

Early Travels and the Idea of European Unity

UNIVERSITY OF TORONTO PRESS
Toronto Buffalo London

© University of Toronto Press Incorporated 2011
Toronto Buffalo London
www.utppublishing.com
Printed in Canada

ISBN 978-1-4426-4310-9

Library and Archives Canada Cataloguing in Publication

Ugland, Trygve, 1969–
Jean Monnet and Canada : early travels and the idea of
European unity / Trygve Ugland.

(European Union studies series)
Includes bibliographical references and index.
ISBN 978-1-4426-4310-9

1. Monnet, Jean, 1888–1979.   2. Monnet, Jean, 1888–1979 –
Travel – Canada.   3. Canada – Civilization – 1867–1914.
4. European Union – History.   5. Hudson's Bay Company
– Employees – Biography.   6. Statesmen – Europe –
Biography.   I. Title.   II. Series: European Union studies

FC551.M58U45 2011   971.05′6092   C2010-906293-0

University of Toronto Press acknowledges the financial
assistance to its publishing program of the Canada Council
for the Arts and the Ontario Arts Council.

 Canada Council   Conseil des Arts
for the Arts   du Canada

 ONTARIO ARTS COUNCIL
CONSEIL DES ARTS DE L'ONTARIO

University of Toronto Press acknowledges the financial
support of the Government of Canada through the Canada
Book Fund for its publishing activities.

Dedicated to my family in Norway,
to my wife Catherine, who attracted me to North America,
and to our wonderful daughters, Clara and Léa,
who draw inspiration from both the Old World and the New World

Contents

FOREWORD BY ROGER MORGAN   ix
PREFACE   xiii

1 Travelling and Political Inspiration   3
2 A New World in Canada and a New Theory for
   Europe   16
3 Monnet and the Hudson's Bay Company   33
4 Monnet's Canadian Scheme in Preparation for the
   Second World War   52
5 Canada as Monnet's Early Inspiration and Lifelong
   Liaison   69

CHRONOLOGY   85
NOTES   87
REFERENCES   95
INDEX   103

Illustrations follow page 46

Foreword

The great Frenchman Jean Monnet (1888–1979) must count as one of the most influential public figures of the twentieth century. Without Monnet's initiative in 1950 in getting the French Foreign Minister Robert Schuman to propose the Monnet-designed 'Schuman Plan' for pooling Western Europe's coal and steel resources, it is unlikely that the European Union of today would have come into existence.

This dramatic event was, however, only one incident in a career packed with creative achievements. As Trygve Ugland's survey of it reminds us, the First World War saw Jean Monnet occupying a key position in wartime economic planning by France and her allies. He then became the deputy secretary-general of the newly founded League of Nations for the first three years of its existence, before moving on to become an international investment banker. In this capacity he undertook large-scale financial operations in Poland, Romania, China, and elsewhere, becoming (briefly) a millionaire by the early 1930s. In the Second World War he again played a crucial role in allied economic planning, first organizing aircraft production for France in Canada and then representing both France and the United Kingdom in Washington. In post-war France, as the dynamic and successful head of the national economic planning agency, he was well placed to steer the French government into creating the European Coal and Steel Community, of

which Monnet was the executive head from 1952 to 1955.
In 1976, after another two decades of activism in the cause
of European unity, he was honoured by the decision of the
European Community's political leaders to make him the
first honorary citizen of Europe.

Trygve Ugland's short but stimulating book focuses on
an aspect of Monnet's life and work that earlier writers
have downplayed or even ignored: the influence exercised
on him by his intensive experience of Canada in the years
between 1907 and 1914. As an eighteen-year-old, already
fluent in English after a two-year stay in London, Monnet
arrived in the booming city of Winnipeg as a salesman for
the brandy produced by his father's firm. By 1911, after
travelling the length and breadth of Canada, he landed a
contract with the Hudson's Bay Company that made the
Monnet firm the HBC's exclusive supplier of brandy for
the entire area from Fort William to Vancouver Island. As
Trygve Ugland shows, Monnet's high-level contacts with the
HBC led to Canada's playing a large part in his strategic
operations during both world wars.

Trygve Ugland explores the interesting idea that Monnet's experience of Canada, coming at an impressionable
age, must have done much to shape his approach to projects and undertakings in general, and thus to the impressive achievements of his later years, particularly in the
institutional 'construction of Europe.' The book provides
considerable support for this view. We read, for instance,
that the eminent American economist and government
official Walt Rostow, who worked closely on designing
the European Coal and Steel Community with Monnet,
thought that the latter had been inspired by his experience
of Canadians' commitment to progress and innovation 'to
think systematically in dynamic terms of change as a natural
condition.'

Some of Trygve Ugland's suggestions about the extent of
Canada's influence on Monnet are more speculative. Certainly we should not lose sight of all the other formative

experiences of his eventful life – not least his time as a top official of the League of Nations – but Ugland argues persuasively that the Canadian dimension must have counted for a great deal. Monnet must have been impressed by the pervasive spirit of enterprise he encountered in the rapidly expanding city of Winnipeg, which seemed to him to transform immigrants from Europe; again, by the experience of trust and cooperation even between strangers (as when a rural blacksmith spontaneously lent the young Frenchman his horse); and by the way in which the Canadian federal constitution shared power effectively between the national capital and the provinces. All these must have helped to shape Monnet's sense of how human capacities could be encouraged by well-designed institutions and to inspire him to create such institutions for Europe.

Trygve Ugland's book makes a welcome contribution to our understanding of Jean Monnet's approach to life, of the nature of Canadian society, and of the links between the two.

Roger Morgan
Former Professor of Political Science
European University Institute, Florence

Preface

'I have taken more out of alcohol than alcohol has taken out of me' (Kelly and Smyer-Kelly 2008, 318). These famous words from Winston Churchill have a significant importance to me. Alcohol has many purposes. It can be used as fuel for engines, disinfectants, and solvents, or simply as the partial content of beverages for pleasure and recreation. What is not so well known is that alcohol can provide an academic career for a political scientist. After all, alcohol has provided me a window to study human and organizational behaviour.

My PhD dissertation, published almost a decade ago, discusses how the health and social policy–oriented alcohol control policies of the Nordic countries were affected in the meeting with the European Union during the 1990s. The encounter brought together two distinctive and opposing cultural traditions and historical experiences with alcohol. While alcoholic beverages in most EU member states have traditionally been treated as ordinary consumer products, Finland and Sweden have, since the early twentieth century, treated them as risk factors subject to strict government control.

Alcohol also plays a central role in this book on Jean Monnet, the 'father of Europe.' Although Monnet was never much of a drinker himself, he could certainly subscribe to Churchill's statement. For Jean Monnet, his project of

uniting Europe after the Second World War is strongly related to his early career as a merchant of quality cognac. This
book illustrates how his encounters with the New World in
Canada, while representing his father's cognac company,
played a vital role, as inspiration and enduring reference
point, in his project of uniting the Old World.

In addition to alcohol, Europe has always been the primary focus in my studies, writings, and research projects.
The present study illustrates how Europe has shaped and
been shaped by outside forces, not by ineluctable forces
such as globalization, but by a great man – a leader and a
statesman, buttressed by his early relationship with Canada.
This book illustrates how Jean Monnet saw the future of
Europe in Canada through encounters with newly arrived
European immigrants at the turn of the twentieth century.

There is an abundance of hard evidence to demonstrate
that Monnet was affected by his early experiences in Canada. But it has never been entirely clear precisely how and
in what ways Monnet was inspired by his Canadian voyages.
Accordingly, I have tried to insert his Canadian experiences
in historical context by relating them largely to circumstan-
tial evidence, much in the same way a capable prosecutor,
fully trained in evidentiary procedure, would make a convincing case before a judge and a jury.

The Canadian federation certainly served as inspirational
model. However, it was not the way Canada had organized
the relationship between levels of government that constituted the most important inspiration for Monnet, but rather the optimism he observed in the new economic union
among economically and ethnically diverse people. Monnet realized that Canada's Confederation was a practical
and business-like arrangement that could foster prosperity.
Put otherwise, it was Canada's horizontal integration, not
its vertical integration, along with its apparent economic
well-being, that appears to have inspired Monnet.

In reconstructing this important part of both Canadian
and European history, this study draws on a wide variety of

empirical sources. Monnet did not keep a journal or diary – an omission he regretted as an octogenarian when he began to write his memoirs – but he was a devoted writer of letters and notes. Although I have been granted access to a wide selection of published (Rieben, Camperio-Tixier, and Nicod 2004) and unpublished notes, relatively few letters from Monnet's early life are still available. Most of the letters Monnet wrote to his family from his early journeys abroad were burnt during the Second World War, when the Nazis established headquarters at the family house in Cognac. Nonetheless, Monnet as a theorist-in-making can be gleaned from other sources, and in particular from his own memoirs with their notable observations and reflections on Canada. According to European integration expert and Monnet's long-time friend François Fontaine, who also collaborated with Monnet to write his life story, only events that had a 'durable significance' (1991a, 26) and that 'illustrated his thinking' (20) were included in details in the memoirs.

This study also relies on unpublished documents, correspondence, and original historical data extracted from archives both in Canada and in Europe. I am grateful to Françoise Nicod, head of the Jean Monnet Foundation for Europe Archives, for her advice and assistance during my research trip to Lausanne, Switzerland, during the summer of 2008, as well as to Denise Jones and Debra Moore at the Hudson's Bay Company Archives in Winnipeg, Manitoba. Thanks also to Eric Roussel for allowing me access to central documents from the Hennessy Archives in Cognac, France, and to John Boylan (Public Archives and Records Office of Prince Edward Island), Jonathan H. Davidson (Provincial Archives of Alberta), Julien Gascard (Maison de Jean Monnet), Christopher Kotecki (Archives of Manitoba), Richard Leliévre (Library and Archives Canada), Florence Le Marhollec (Thomas Hine & Co.) and Tim Novak (Saskatchewan Archives Board) for providing useful information and resources.

I appreciate the welcome that the Jean Monnet Association gave me to Monnet's old farm-home, Houjarray, in the *département* of Yvelines, southwest of Paris. Houjarray – which the former cognac producer and salesman ironically bought from the well-known Swedish physician and temperance advocate Ivan Bratt in 1945 – is now a popular museum with more than ten thousand visitors a year. Thanks are also due to Jack Germain-Robin, who provided me with important background knowledge of the town of Cognac, where Monnet's memory is still kept very much alive; to Pierre Guerette for taking the original photographs in this book; and to the Jean Monnet Foundation for Europe Archives in Lausanne and the Norway Heritage for giving me the permission to use some of their photographs.

Thanks also for the constructive comments I have received from Morten Egeberg (University of Oslo), Clifford P. Hackett (Jean Monnet Council in Washington), Heather McKeen-Edwards (Bishop's University), Johan P. Olsen (University of Oslo), and the participants at the Seventh Biennial Conference of the European Community Studies Association in Edmonton, Alberta, where I presented an award-winning paper on Jean Monnet and his Canadian inspiration in September 2008. In addition to the valuable suggestions I received from the conference participants, I was encouraged by the two editors of this University of Toronto Press book series on European Union Studies, Jeffrey Kopstein and Amy Verdun, to write this book. My heartfelt gratitude goes to the European Commission, whose generous grant contributed greatly to this book series, and to the acquisitions editor at the University of Toronto Press, Daniel Quinlan, who most skilfully steered the manuscript through the various stages of publication. I was also genuinely pleased and grateful to receive thoughtful comments from three anonymous scholars on an earlier version of this manuscript.

Besides continued financial support from the Social Sciences and Humanities Research Council of Canada, I also wish to thanks Bishop's University, which provides a favourable environment conducive to research, writing, and teaching on European politics. Bishop's University's generosity is also gratefully acknowledged for providing additional funding of this project on Jean Monnet through research, travel, and publication grants. I am also very much indebted to my first 'academic editor' and colleague from the Department of Political Studies at Bishop's University, Andrew F. Johnson, for his consultation, especially in relation to Canadian history and politics, as well as in relation to literary style and matters of expression. An unusually dull and rain-soaked spring and summer of 2009 in Sherbrooke, Quebec, was brightened by our lengthy discussions on European and Canadian politics and on Jean Monnet's role in them.

And finally, I have dedicated this book to my family in Norway, my wife Catherine, and our daughters Clara and Léa, for their love and inspiration.

Trygve Ugland
Sherbrooke, 5 May 2010

JEAN MONNET AND CANADA:
EARLY TRAVELS AND THE IDEA OF
EUROPEAN UNITY

1

Travelling and Political Inspiration

I went to Winnipeg to visit our clients, tough men in a tough climate, up against forces of nature that were rewarding but piti-
less to the weak. These men were sensitive to the fine quality of
cognac. They demanded the best. But if we talked about cognac,
they asked me little about Cognac. What was going on in Europe had no interest for these Europeans making the West, turning their backs on the Old World. Their efforts, their vision of a
broader, richer future, that was what we talked about nearly all
the time. I soaked myself in these new impressions.

Jean Monnet (1978, 44)

First impressions tend to be long lasting but rarely as enduring as Jean Monnet's impressions of Winnipeg in 1907.
Monnet was not even twenty years old and on his first long
voyage. He, like most in their late teens, must have been
awestruck by what he saw: a flourishing city, situated in the
desolate magnificence of the Canadian prairies, and above
all, a city holding immense economic hope for the future,
even from the perspective of immigrant workers, toiling in
harsh circumstances. It is reasonable to assume that Monnet, as an impressionable youth, carried their visions and
expectations for prosperity with him throughout his life.
The assumption will be given empirical substance in this
volume as will an equally reasonable assumption: that Monnet, as a matter-of-fact young man, in training by his father

for a career in business, must have been able to quickly
identify the source of Winnipeg's prosperity, namely Canada's economic union of 1867.

Canada's Confederation, a practical and business-like
arrangement among the former colonies, had established
the infrastructure necessary to support and sustain the
Wheat Boom (1896–1913). And Monnet arrived in its midst
and specifically at its centre of gravity, Winnipeg. If an economic union, a marriage of convenience among economically and ethnically diverse colonies, could foster riches,
it would seem plausible that, from Monnet's Canadian
experiences, similar practical arrangements could generate
and sustain affluence in Europe half a century later.

Monnet seemed to realize from his Canadian travels
that interstate economic unions and invention share the
same biological mother: necessity – the kind of necessity
that 'leaves no room for hesitation,' Monnet would remark
much later in life (1978, 35). To be sure, Canada's economic union, the Canadian Confederation, 'was made possible
by a remarkable conjuncture of events which brought each
of the separate colonies to a crisis in its affairs at the same
time and pointed to a political union as a common solution to their difficulties' (Smiley 1978, 9). War – the threat
of US imperial expansion – and economic necessity – the
near bankruptcy of the colonies and the removal of British
preferential tariffs – were the primary factors that created
the Canadian confederation in 1867. These are not neces-
sarily factors that Monnet considered from his youth until
his adult life. But then early impressions, coupled with economic and political savvy, based on experience, are likely to
have been major considerations for Monnet when, in the
aftermath of war and a potential war – the aftermath of the
Second World War and the new Soviet threat – and its con-
sequential dire economic consequences for Continental
Europeans, he forged the European Coal and Steel Community (ECSC), the genesis of a new European confederation, now known as the European Union (EU).

The Canadian political model, with its attendant successful economic consequences, would not have been lost on Monnet, especially because he had been dispatched to obtain his education by way of practical experience and observation in Canada. He learned his lessons well. He clearly understood the necessity of practical arrangements to forge and sustain economic development. However, Monnet's practical and business-like approach, an approach likely derived from his Canadian impressions, to matters of industrial infrastructure – coal and steel – and ultimately to matters of state, could have been accommodated only in a culture of political invention and experimentation. Europe has been the prototypical representation of that culture, as Samuel Finer (1997) concluded in his comprehensive overview of the history of government by explaining that historically, Europe, as a whole, has traditionally been a fertile region for innovation in ideology and in forms of governance. After all, Europe is a political scientist's laboratory for the study of political invention. In the long course of European history and especially during the last two centuries, every type of ideology and government, from left to right, and interstate union, from confederation to federation to centralization, has been tested in the European laboratory. One broad conclusion can be drawn from the tests: Europeans are receptive to political experimentation and mercilessly quick to dismiss an arrangement if it does not work. Accordingly, the relative longevity of the European Union is a testament to its future durability, despite the numerous challenges that the member states and the union collectively are facing daily. Its longevity – and success – has been wrought by necessity and spearheaded by practical, if brilliant, statesmanship. After all, Europe has a long history of launching economic and defensive multi-state unions, most of which have been fragile and transient.

Many attempts – both peaceful and violent – have been made at creating a politically integrated Europe across the centuries. The French humanist and writer Pierre Dubois' political pamphlets promoting the establishment of a European confederation to be ruled by a 'European council' of 'wise, expert and faithful men' at the beginning of the fourteenth century represent one of the earliest (Mayne 1962, 36). Adolf Hitler's dream of European unity under 'ein Volk, ein Reich, ein Führer' (Ryback 1996) represents a more recent and horrific attempt. Among all the initiatives, however, the 1951 Treaty of Paris establishing the European Coal and Steel Community, which over time evolved into today's European Union, stands out as a remarkably successful case of deliberate political design (Ugland 2009). Jean Monnet saw international cooperation as the only means of survival for a Europe emerging from the ruins of the Second World War, and although he worked closely with other people, Monnet is recognized as, among other things, architect and master builder (Ball 1978, 25), creator and instigator (Yergin and Stanislaw 1998), entrepreneur and planner (Ardagh 1968), and innovator and trailblazer (Rostow 1994) for European post-war unity. In 1950, *Newsweek* displayed his photograph on the front cover of its 19 June issue. The caption read, 'Monnet: Europe's No. 1 Idea Man.'

The processes of institution-building, lawmaking, policy integration, and market creation in the EU represent a decisive rupture with Europe's past. Moreover, the EU has become a model of internationalization with distinct characteristics (Laffan 1998). The EU represents a form of 'deep' regionalism in contrast to other regional arrangements in the world such as the North American Free Trade Agreement, Asia Pacific Economic Co-operation, the Association of Southeast Asian Nations, the African Union, and the Southern Common Market, to mention a few. The EU is 'deep' in contrast to 'shallow' forms of regionalism in the sense that no other regionalism in the international system is characterized by equivalent ties, in either profundity or breadth, and no other regionalism has displayed the potential to alter the relative congruence of territory, identity, and function, which characterizes the nation-state. Despite its economic objectives, the EU project from the outset was supported by strong normative underpinnings related to the urgent needs to tame the dark side of European nationalism, in order to achieve lasting peace, and that adds to its distinctiveness (Laffan 1998).

All in all, the EU is considered to be the most remarkable international political integration project the world has ever witnessed. And Jean Monnet is its father. In 1976, the European heads of state and government celebrated this paternity by distinguishing him as the first honorary citizen of Europe. Additional tributes followed: in 1986, the European Parliament decided to mount an exhibition on the life of Jean Monnet, under the name of 'Father of the European Community,' at his house Houjarray, which the European Parliament had recently purchased and restored. A year later, former colleagues and close friends formed the Jean Monnet Association, whose goal is to contribute its support for all activities and projects aimed at reviving and transmitting the memory of Jean Monnet, his work and his teachings.[1] On the occasion of the 100th anniversary of his birth, the EU decreed 1988 the Jean Monnet European Year, and over the years, more than a thousand French and European cities have named public places after Jean Monnet. Homage to his talent, skills, and vision has even been paid abroad. In 2006, *Time* magazine included Monnet in the '60 Years of Heroes' list and identified him as one of the most 'influential leaders and revolutionaries' in Europe after the Second World War.

Recipients of eminent honours and awards tend to become centres of attention and adulatory curiosity, and Jean Monnet's life and work is no exception. For instance, François Duchêne (1994) portrays Monnet's political career with an insider's eye, as he worked closely with Monnet for more than a decade. Two years later, Éric Roussel (1996) presented readers of French with a lengthy and authoritative account of Monnet's life. But despite the breadth and depth of these biographies, and others, one significant aspect of Monnet's life has not been fully explored.

It is well known that Monnet had a special relationship with North America and its people. While Jean Monnet's links with the United States are well covered (Hackett 1995b), his many important encounters with Canada have been given scant attention except by Monnet himself. Monnet's *Memoirs* tell us that he visited Canada on numerous occasions, and that he developed a comprehensive network of contacts with Canadians in many provinces and territories over many years (Monnet 1976, 1978). Although Monnet argued that his experiences in Canada were an inspiration for him in his lifelong zeal for European political integration, the details and consequences of these encounters have not been systematically analysed. This is, of course, the primary purpose of this book, but to do so, informed by theory.

Theory, in an academic sense, was of little concern to Jean Monnet. He was never a member of the intelligentsia; he hardly read books, and he disliked political and economic theory (Fontaine 1991a; Fransen 2001). There are, for instance, very few references to theoretical exposition or even to books, for that matter, in his memoirs. Duchêne (1991) characterizes him as a man who placed a high value on simplicity, and who avoided intellectual adornments that might complicate and distort essential messages in his communications. As a result, Monnet has generally been depicted as a practical and technocratic political figure rather than as a theoretician (Bromberger and Bromberger 1969; Duchêne 1991, 1994; Joly 2007). Nevertheless, Monnet's detailed recollections of Canada are rich in theoretical code and content, as was his vision of European supranational unity. Accordingly, the case is made in subsequent chapters that Monnet's 'theory' emerged from Canada, where his early observations and experiences were transformed into an epiphany for the future of Europe.

Travelling and Political Theory

A 'theory' does not emerge from a single experience. It is formed by an accumulation of life experiences, of which travel is thought to contribute a vital ingredient. To this day, travel is considered crucial to a person's development, and particularly to young persons' intellectual growth and maturation. Indeed, it is common and acceptable for young people – or at least those from middle- and upper-level income backgrounds – to take a year off to travel, upon completion of a basic formal education. To be sure, some of us, as educators at the post-secondary level, even encourage our students to apply for international educational exchanges or international internships so that they can learn from experiences that we cannot provide in the classroom. Thus, the intimate relationship between travelling and political theory has been given much attention. This linkage is addressed in the following pages. However, the link is not entirely a modern concept.

The word *theory* comes from the Greek *theoria* and the verb *theorein*, which means 'to see or to observe' (Bill 1901; Rawlinson 1859). *Theoria* also has associated meanings that refer to different modes of seeing or observing, like journey or spectacle (public festival). Furthermore, *theorist* derives from the Greek *theoros*, which was the name for an emissary who travelled on behalf of his city to other cities or societies to observe their rituals. Herodotus, 'the father of history' (Thompson 1996), refers to a trip that Solon made to Lydia and Egypt to learn about other peoples as *theoria* (Redfield 1985; Rutherford 2000, 135). In this story, travelling is linked to political wisdom and theory.

According to Sheldon S. Wolin (2001), *theoria* takes the form of a story told by a traveller who has recently returned from a journey to a distant and hitherto unknown land. Typically the traveller describes the people of that place as happy, peaceful, economically self-sufficient, and virtuous because of their exemplary institutions and beliefs. The traveller's description serves the triple purpose of explanation, criticism, and prescription:

He shows the causes that have produced the ideal condition and he identifies the principles (e.g., abolition of private property) behind those causes. The essence of utopias is that they should embody extractable principles, which can then be turned back upon the society from whence the journeyer has come: uncannily, virtually every feature of the discovered society, it is revealed, embodies a prescription or principle that can remedy the perceived ills of the traveler's homeland. (Wolin 2001, 35)

Political theorists have always been great journeyers, and their theories are often direct results of empirical observations made during travels. Wolin (2001) considers the renowned French traveller and political theorist Alexis de Tocqueville as a traveller whose theory is based on what he saw and experienced on his journeys. Just as Tocqueville's journey to America in 1831 convinced him that he had witnessed the future (Tocqueville 2000), it appears that Monnet's trip to Canada in 1907 formed the quintessential core of the inspiration for his lifelong fixation on European supranational unity. Although their approaches were different in a number of ways, comparisons between Tocqueville's and Monnet's encounters with America can be made. As an anecdote, it can be mentioned that, although Monnet did not seem to have any particular interest in books, he once gave a leather-bound copy, in French, of Tocqueville's *Democracy in America* as a gift to the American anti-trust lawyer Robert Bowie, with whom he worked closely during the ECSC negotiations.[2] However, Monnet does not make any reference to this thoughtful and highly symbolic gift or to Tocqueville in his *Memoirs*.

Jean Monnet was an inveterate traveller and he lived a large part of his life abroad. In addition to his travels to North America, Monnet had already visited Bulgaria,

China, Egypt, England, Greece, Poland, Romania, Russia, and Sweden before the Second World War broke out. His trip to Canada was his first long voyage, and certainly also the most ground-breaking.

However, what separates a regular traveller from a *theorist*, and a travelogue from a *theoria*? According Wolin (2001), a *theorist* relies on the method of comparison and seeks to draw lessons from the similarities and differences observed. A *theoria* is formed when the disparate empirical observations are elevated to an abstract plane and into a conceptual whole. While it is generally acknowledged that Tocqueville and his theory of democracy fulfils the criteria for *theorist* and *theoria*, respectively, the book illustrates why Monnet should be considered a significant theorist in terms of his own theory, although unbeknownst to him, in the context of historical theory.

Placing Politics in Time

True to its title, *Jean Monnet and Canada: Early Travels and the Idea of European Unity*, this book explains the relationship between Monnet's encounters with Canada and Canadians and his political project of uniting Europe. It also relates how his Canadian experiences inspired and spurred him to promote European political integration throughout his entire career. Monnet's early trip to Canada convinced him that it was possible to achieve a lasting political change from the narrow-minded nationalism that had plagued Europe throughout the centuries. And Canada became a source of creativity, both as an inspirational model and as a guiding reference for him in times of turmoil and conflict.

However, the linkage between Monnet's trip to Canada in 1907 and the establishment of Monnet's ECSC proposal in 1950 cannot, and should not, be interpreted as a direct causal link. Connections among experiences, inspiration, and personal 'theory' tend to be tenuous in current political analysis. The battle between Straussian political theorists and political scientists qua scientists has long since abated and, through sheer exhaustion, both sides have allowed each other to coexist peacefully (Almond 1990). Nevertheless, historical analysis of political phenomena, occupying the middle ground between the two rivals, seems somehow to have become a threatened species situated between a rock and a hard place, because the approach involves both empirical and interpretive generalizations. However, the explanation of complex social dynamics requires facts, as well as an acceptance of values. Put otherwise, 'history matters,' according to Pierson (2004), who argues persuasively that his 'placing politics in time' approach to political phenomena enriches explanations of complex social dynamics.

Pierson's approach is formally designated as 'historical institutionalism' because he and others evaluate factors – among which ideas are crucial – in explaining the gradual evolution of political institutions. The relevance of history is also emphasized in other variants of institutionalism, where political development is seen as a result of organic growth and historic drift or evolution. By comparison, many political scientists tend to focus on processes of immediate cause and effects of events, thus normally capturing a 'snapshot' of reality in contrast to slowly elucidating and illuminating the storyline of a 'movie' (Pierson 2004). Both require meticulous and methodological rigour, albeit of a different sort. But the former tend to be less subject to interpretation than the latter, if for no other reason – and there tend to be others – than length. There are an awful lot of snapshots in a two-hour movie.

Snapshots, such as explaining political phenomena on the basis of statistical associations among precisely 'operationalized' independent and dependent variables, are compelling and worthwhile, as are reasonably accurate assessments of causes or effects of a specific public policy. The same can be said of other empirically oriented sub-fields that can boast methodological sophistication. But there are other problems and processes of significance and, above all, integral to the study of politics that require a looser, but still scrupulous, more qualitatively oriented approach. The creation and development of political institutions is a case in point. Many 'institutionalists' make this case, and so do I in respect, not just to ideas, but in relation to one outstanding purveyor of an idea: Jean Monnet.

Monnet's early life is interesting in itself as an independent object of inquiry. More importantly, it is more than just interesting. It is instructive – and absorbing – insofar as it enhances our understanding of the processes and outcomes of post-war attempts at radical supranational political design at the European level and particularly of the role of individual actors in forging and sustaining that design. But such understanding requires considerably more than a snapshot.

The successful establishment of the European Coal and Steel Community was in large part due to Jean Monnet's extraordinary ability to identify and exploit available spaces for institutional design (Ugland 2009). His proposal received almost immediate preliminary approval by the six participating states: Belgium, France, Germany, Italy, Luxembourg, and the Netherlands. The formal negotiations started less than two months after the idea had been presented for the first time in May 1950. The final treaty was signed in April 1951, less than a year after the formal negotiations had commenced. The ECSC came into effect in August 1952 after having been ratified by the national parliaments of the six member states. Although several elements of Monnet's original vision did not survive unaltered in the final treaty, his achievements represent a powerful example of deliberate political design.

In all of these achievements, Monnet's views on contexts and procedures associated with successful political and institutional design were influenced by his early encounters with Canada and Canadians. However, institution-building is a social process that unfolds over time, and change in the European political order seems to be an artefact of a complex ecology of processes and trajectories, rather than the result of a single dominant process (Olsen 2007). However, this complexity does not mean that political scientists should refrain from attempts to develop claims about temporal connections between events in European politics, or elsewhere. In this, as in similar cases, we are required to retroactively immerse ourselves in the social, cultural, and political distance that separates us from our subject by more than one hundred years on his first visit to Canada and into the subsequent half century that it took to realize his vision. Our immersion provides us with clues to enable us to think as Jean Monnet might have thought in connecting and interpreting historical circumstances to conception, vision, and ultimately to realization.

So what is the connection between Monnet's early encounters with Canada and Canadians, and the creation as well as the development of the European Union? Let the scenes unfold as in a 'moving picture,' but by way of chapter-by-chapter that together constitute an integrated spellbinding story of one man's contribution to peace and prosperity.

Chapter Overview

The book is organized into five parts. While the first chapter provides a theoretical context, chapter 2 describes the Canada Monnet met in 1907 and the impressions he drew from it. In particular, this chapter forms the linkage between Jean Monnet's first meeting with the New World in Canada and his new theory for Europe. Subsequent chapters strengthen this linkage. In chapter 3, attention is turned to the extended period Monnet spent in Canada between 1907 and 1914, and its long-lasting consequences. Above all, Monnet's enduring association with the Hudson's Bay Company – a company so closely linked to the birth of Canada itself – is explored. In fact, this company not only saved the Monnet family cognac company on several occasions, but Monnet also relied on the friendly relations he had developed with the Hudson's Bay Company to promote the interests of Allied supplies – and ultimately to save Europe – during the First World War. Monnet's relationship and links to Canada were also evident during the Second World War, and chapter 4 provides an astounding illustration of Monnet's creativity, inventiveness, and optimism when his Canadian scheme to rearm Europe against the Nazi aggressors was presented to the American president, Franklin Delano Roosevelt. Chapter 5 examines the relationship between Monnet's two worlds, Europe and North America. Although Jean Monnet used the concepts of 'Old World' versus 'New World' to describe the two, he always treated them as equals and as partners in a common project: world peace. In fact, Monnet argued for the creation of a far-reaching 'Atlantic community' in which European nations together with Canada and the United States would share common institutions based on true delegation of powers. In light of these discussions, but also based on the intimate links between Jean Monnet and Canada, this chapter also elaborates on the status of contemporary Canada–EU relations and on the legacy of Jean Monnet in Canada.

2

A New World in Canada and a
New Theory for Europe

J'aime beaucoup votre pays. En fait, voilà plus de 50 ans que pour
la première fois, je suis arrivé à Québec en bateau, et que j'ai tra-
versé alors votre beau pays, ce que j'ai fait plusieurs fois depuis.

Jean Monnet to Pierre Dupuy,
Canadian Ambassador to France, 5 December 1962[3]

So it appears that the initial frame in the story of Jean Monnet's connection to Canada was a fond memory. Fond memories are much like cognac: they get better with age. But in
the parlance of the young cognac salesman, his first trip to
Canada must have seemed like an 'extra old' premier cru
– the very best among cognacs – from the beginning to the
end of his sojourn. And eventually it became an elixir to
transform a divided Europe into a consensual whole.

Monnet was sufficiently fortunate to embark on his journey at the dawn of the Golden Age of Travel, when marvel-
lous passenger ships, capable of transporting up to 1,400
passengers, travelled the oceans. The SS *Virginian* was much
like other Allan Line ships, easily identified by an imposing
black funnel, ringed by a striking white loop near the top.
But it stood out among other ships of its distinguished class
in that it sported two masts and three screws, and could
travel up to eighteen knots an hour, four to five knots faster
than sister ships. As a matter of fact, in 1906, a year after
its maiden voyage, the SS *Virginian* set a new world record

of five days, twenty hours, and forty minutes for the voyage from Liverpool to Quebec (Bonsor 1980, 5:1883). It is on this spectacular ship that Jean Monnet embarked on his first long voyage on 19 July 1907.[4]

Monnet, just four months shy of his nineteenth birthday, must have been as excited about his trip on this marvel of technology as any teenager would have been some fifty years later boarding the supersonic Concorde for a first transatlantic voyage. The ship, like the Concorde, was a testament to the ability of humankind to develop and master new technologies – and ideas – that could change the way nations communicate and interrelate with each other. However, travel on the SS *Virginian* would have been infinitely more extraordinary to Monnet than setting off on today's equivalent of the modern middle-class student's year off, because he found himself in the intimate company of mainly famous, sophisticated, and, above all, wealthy adults. Monnet travelled on a first-class ticket and so he would have been reasonably familiar with most of the other 136 saloon (first-class) passengers, separated by cabins, dining areas, and even decks from the 1,199 second- and third-class passengers on board.

On a ship, even on modern cruise ships, passengers dine together for days and get to know each other well, an experience considerably more personal than taking a modern flight, and more enlightening for a young man. However, in 1907 passengers were entirely segregated by class, that is, by the price paid for a ticket, and so young Monnet would have been rubbing shoulders daily with the rich and famous. For example, the renowned American actor Richard Mansfield was onboard SS *Virginian* on this voyage.[5]

There is no evidence that Jean Monnet met Mr Mansfield, but just being in the company of such luminaries must have been edifying for a young man. However, it is not as if Monnet were an insular youth. Quite the contrary: throughout his life he had encountered all sorts of strangers from different nations. Clients from America, Britain, Germany, and Scandinavia frequently visited the family company in Cognac, but still, they were business associates. Monnet was certainly not sophisticated or schooled in the ways of the world, and he was not well-educated in a formal sense. His father seemed to think that the best education was derived from life experiences.

Jean Monnet was born into a family of brandy merchants in 1888 in Cognac, a small town with approximately twenty thousand inhabitants on the Charente River 465 kilometres southwest of Paris. However small, its premium quality brandies have brought world renown to Cognac since the seventeenth century. Hennessy, Martell, and Rémy Martin are among the largest and most famous distilleries of this nectar referred to by Victor Hugo as 'la liqueur des dieux.' However, in 1838, a large number of smaller vineyard owners of the Cognac Country united and founded the United Vineyard Proprietors Company (UVPC) as a joint stock company in order to compete with the larger ones. In 1897, Jean Monnet's father, Jean-Gabriel Monnet, became the director of the UVPC, and not long after, he acquired a controlling amount of the shares. He put his name on the bottle labels from 1901, and the products were from thenceforth known as J.G. Monnet & Co. Cognac. The company was owned by Monnet's family until 1963, when it was sold to a German company, Scharlachberg.[6]

It has been said about Jean-Gabriel Monnet that he was a 'Prince Charming whose one great aim in life was to see Monnet brandy cover the earth' (Davenport 1944, 122). Over the years, J.G. Monnet & Co. cognacs won numerous national and international awards, and the salamander that Jean-Gabriel Monnet selected as an emblem for the company became a symbol of premier quality worldwide. The senior Monnet's ambitious objective could not have been realized without the help of his son, Jean, and his hard work in Canada, as revealed in the following pages.

'Travelling' or 'seeing the world' were not expressions heard often in Cognac. Instead, residents spoke of 'visiting clients' (Monnet 1978). Jean Monnet and his younger brother, Gaston, were sent out at an early age to maintain old business and develop new business networks for the company.[7] Formal education was not a priority in the family, and Jean Monnet had shown little intellectual promise and enthusiasm for school: 'I had never liked school. I would not, or could not for some reason, learn bookish knowledge by heart' (Monnet 1978, 38). In 1904, at the age of sixteen, Monnet left school for good and was sent to London, England, to learn 'not only the language of our most important clients, but also their habits and their ways of doing business' (44). His two-year apprenticeship in London at an agent for J.G. Monnet & Co. Cognac prepared him well for more distant travels.

Thus, when Monnet came aboard the SS *Virginian* on 19 July 1907 on his way to Canada, he must have felt as if he had come upon something exhilarating to all of his senses, something like an excellent cognac. The slow-paced traditional and very practical background – fermenting and selling cognac – must have stood in stark contrast to the rushed ultra-modern majesty of the ship and to the elegance of his accommodations and his fellow passengers in Saloon class. But he did not say so in his memoirs, just as he did not disclose the exact date of his departure. As a result, the precise departure and arrival dates, along with his travel route, have been a matter of speculation (Hackett 2008). At best, Monnet indicates that he was eighteen years old when he left, and so it has been assumed that he travelled to Canada in 1906 because he was born in November 1888. However, his name is not among the passengers travelling from Europe to Canada in November or December 1906. Instead, scrutiny of passenger lists reveals that what was most probably his first North American arrival was in Montreal via Quebec City from Liverpool on Friday, 26 July 1907.[8] He was aged eighteen years and 258 days when he arrived aboard the SS *Virginian* of the Allan Line Steamship Company.

However much he was impressed with his new surround-
ings in late July 1907, he went with an open mind. For Monnet, this voyage was not a theoretical project related to
finding a vision that would later materialize as European
political integration. It was purely a practical business venture. In fact, upon his departure, Monnet's father advised
him, 'Don't take any books with you. No one can do your
thinking for you' (Monnet 1978, 44). Although not stating
it explicitly, his father indirectly encouraged Monnet to
put the Old World behind him and meet the New World
with open eyes. Monnet must have followed this advice
and, without any intention, the journey, from beginning to
end, served as inspiration for his theory of European supranational unity.

The New World in Canada

Canada was the next frame in which Monnet emerged. In
Quebec City, Monnet would have witnessed an essential
ingredient in the spirit of the New World. He could not have
helped but notice the nearly complete monumental Quebec
Bridge that was cantilevering across the St Lawrence River
– a major engineering feat of its time. Regrettably, he could
not have missed the tragic news about its collapse, killing
seventy-five workers, during the month after his arrival. But
then again, he must also have sensed the unbounded optimism that inspired efforts to begin reconstruction after the
collapse.[9] Such events make impressions on travellers and
tend to support the adage that travel develops a person's
mind, especially the imagination.

But Monnet came to Canada not as a tourist but as a businessman. His voyage was focused on the search for emerging markets in Western Canada where the bigger and more
renowned brandy firms from Cognac had not extended
their reach (Fontaine 1991a). However, his trip was also
motivated by the desire to expand the important relation-

ship between the UVPC and the Hudson's Bay Company (HBC) that had been established in 1896.[10]

Monnet could not have happened onto a more robust economic atmosphere than was apparent in Canada at that time. Three years earlier, Prime Minister Wilfrid Laurier had declared the twentieth century to be 'Canada's century' in a speech that is worth quoting at least in part:

The twentieth century shall be the century of Canada and of Canadian development. For the next seventy-five years, nay for the next hundred years, Canada shall be the star towards which all men who love progress and freedom shall come. (Kingwell and Moore 1999, 69)

Moreover, and in the same year, Clifford Sifton, Laurier's minister of the interior and superintendent general of Indian Affairs, had expressed similar sentiments:

We look forward to the production of natural wealth of all kinds ... We expect to see cities and towns springing up, in which all the comforts and refinements of civilization will be within reach of all. We expect to see a creditable system of education amongst our people, in which intellectual advancement and intellectual culture will go hand in hand with material progress. (Kingwell and Moore 1999, 69)

These were not empty campaign promises made by desperate politicians in search of votes. Laurier and Sifton are merely describing the explosive growth Canada was experiencing in almost all areas of social and economic life at the beginning of the twentieth century: gold and a new type of climate-resistant wheat had just been discovered; the railway that already connected the country from coast to coast was expanded and complemented with other transportation networks on the ground and on water; the largest hydroelectric power plant in the world was under construction to support the rapid industrialization; and scientists and inventors flocked to the country to test their inventions.[11] And finally, new immigration policies encouraging Europeans to immigrate and to participate in this adventure were implemented. The discovery of new natural resources, as well as more effective management of existing natural resources, was supported by new technological innovations. This in turn ignited an industrial boom that could meet the rising demand for manufactured goods from an ever-growing and increasingly prosperous population. Jean Monnet encountered progress and optimism for the future in Canada.

Not only had the connections between Europe and America been greatly facilitated through technological advances and public policies – the Canadian Pacific Railway connected Manitoba, Saskatchewan, Alberta, and British Columbia physically and economically to Eastern Canada and Europe. New towns were springing up along the railway's entire length and were transforming the area 'from empty wilderness to a land of promise' (Bellan 1978, 25). The towns were teaming with new arrivals, mostly pioneers and immigrants, and mostly men. Jean Monnet had a ready and willing group to ply with samples of brandy.

The economic, political, and social atmosphere of Winnipeg, in particular, made an ever-lasting impression on Monnet. At the time of his visit in 1907, Winnipeg was in the midst of a tremendous boom. The population grew from 7,985 inhabitants in 1881 to 163,000 in 1916 (Artibise 1975, 130–1), at a growth rate exceeding that of nearly all other Canadian cities. In fact, Winnipeg was ranked the third most populous city in Canada in 1911, having risen from seventeenth in 1881. The chief source of the city's population growth was new migrants. For the period of 1881–1916, almost 80 per cent of Winnipeg's population was born outside Manitoba (137). A significant number of these immigrants were foreign born, and by 1916, Canadian-born persons accounted for less than half of Winnipeg's population. Although those of British descent far outnumbered any other ethnic group, Northern Europeans, from Scandinavia and Germany, constituted another abundant source of immigrants. The influx of Scandinavian-Icelandic immigrants was particularly plentiful immediately after the turn of the century – a phenomenon Monnet noticed:[12]

At Winnipeg, from the station hotel of the Canadian Pacific Railway where I was staying, I saw trainloads of Scandinavian immigrants pulling in. They were not refugees: they were not starving. They had come to hard, rewarding work – the conquest of new lands. The most common type there was not the speculator, but the entrepreneur. For the first time I met a people whose job was not to manage what already existed, but to develop it without stint. No one thought about limits; no one knew where the frontier was. (Monnet 1978, 45)

Winnipeg's stupendous population growth was closely linked to developments in the local economy, which surged at the turn of the century. Capitalization for Winnipeg's manufacturing sector grew from $691,655 in 1881 to nearly $26 million in 1911. Linked to this trend, manufacturers employed 950 people in 1881, and this number grew to 11,565 in 1911 (Artibise 1975, 123). Ruben Bellan claims that the city's spectacular expansion and prosperity fostered a spirit of 'unbound optimism in the future' (Bellan 1978, 81). In this dynamic atmosphere, Monnet discovered a spirit of openness and trust among people with which he was unfamiliar. After a trip from Moose Jaw, Saskatchewan, and then to Medicine Hat, Alberta, Monnet travelled to a place near Calgary, Alberta. There, one event made a very special impression on him:

I wanted to visit some Scandinavian farmers to whom I had an introduction. I asked a blacksmith who was working in front of his forge what means of transportation there were. Without stopping work, he answered there were none. 'But,' he added, pointing to his horse, 'you can always take this animal. When you come back you just hitch him up in the same place.' His confidence was perfectly natural: and if I had shown him how surprised I was, he would certainly been hurt. (Monnet 1978, 46)

The conclusion Monnet drew from this experience was to become far-reaching: in Cognac, 'people are wary of their neighbours and distrust newcomers even more. Here, I encountered a new way of looking at things: individual initiative could be accepted as a contribution to the general good' (Monnet 1978, 45). Monnet was articulating a vision of the French national character at the beginning of the twentieth century that was similar to what historian Herman Lebovics (1992) refers to as the 'true France,' a society that prized traditional rural values and buttressed integral nationalism and hostility to outsiders.

Although Monnet was not explicitly theorizing, his recollections from Canada are rich in theoretical code because he turned everyday observations into empirical-analytic conceptualizations. As it did for Tocqueville seventy-six years earlier, Monnet's travelling taught him to recognize the acute differences between the Old World and the New World and between the past and the future or, more specifically, between being stuck in history and being free to innovate.

Monnet refers to the New World with a rich future as opposed to the old static Europe. He refers to open-minded people as opposed to the distrusting citizens of Europe. Monnet also recollects the 'dynamism of a world on the move' and the 'spontaneity' that he encountered in Canada: 'To my European eyes, this spontaneity looked like confusion; but I very soon ceased to think in those terms. I became convinced that there could be no progress without disorder on the surface' (1978, 46). Again, a parallel can be drawn with Tocqueville, who eulogized the new freedom he discovered in America, 'a society without roots, without memories, without prejudices, without routines, without common ideas, without a national character, more than a hundreds times happier than ours' (see Wolin 2001, 151). Tocqueville also concluded that the result was not anarchy, as many Europeans might have believed (Tocqueville 2000, 85).

The contrasts between what he observed in Canada and in Cognac – and in France and Europe, for that matter – had a lasting effect on Monnet, and it formed his perceptions of 'change.' According to Walt W. Rostow, who worked closely with Monnet while the ECSC was being established, Monnet's observations from Canada produced an almost 'Schumpeterian (or chaos theory) image' of the process of change, and 'encouraged him to think systematically in dynamic terms of change as a normal condition' (1994, 279).[13] It appears then that Monnet was not satisfied with simply identifying distinctions and discrepancies between the New and the Old World, but as a 'theorist' he was also seeking to define, explain, and draw lessons from them. He realized that although human nature remains constant, attitudes and behaviour can be modified by changing the settings in which people live and work. Because those whom Monnet met in Canada were immigrants, newly arrived from Europe, Monnet concluded that change was also possible in Europe – if only the overriding context of people's lives could be modified.

The New Theory for Europe

Although Monnet seems to have been inspired during his trip to Canada in 1907, concrete plans for European supranational unity were not developed until much later. Some European intellectuals adhered to federalism as an institutional means to resolve conflict among people of different backgrounds and different interests, especially after the successful installation of federal systems in the former European colonies of Canada (1867) and Australia (1901). However, visionaries of a united Europe, from the early nineteenth century until the 1930s, were usually utopian idealists who failed to understand the realities of international power politics (Murray and Rich 1996). But it was the reality of the horrific loss of life and concomitant economic devastation in the aftermath of Second World War that transformed visionaries into determined and realistic men of vision. For some, European supranational unity had become a necessity in order to avoid such overwhelming destruction on such an enormous scale again.

Jean Monnet was always a pragmatist and realist. After having completed careers as a cognac merchant, a public servant managing Allied food supplies in the First World War, an international diplomat for the League of Nations, an international investment banker, and then as a senior Allied administrator during the Second World War, Monnet was appointed director of the French Modernization Plan in 1945. It was during his tenure as director that his path-breaking plan for European supranational unity was presented.

After the Second World War, there was widespread feeling that Europe must make concrete plans to avoid future armed conflicts. In the late 1940s, the European Movement was born from such popular sentiment. It was a loose assortment of individuals and interest groups – 'clerical and anti-clerical, right and left, liberal and *dirigiste*, regionalist and multilateralist, "Atlantic" and "third force"' – that shared the idea of European unity (Mayne 1962, 80). However, there was little agreement on the principles on which future European cooperation and unity should be based. A clear split could be observed between the 'unionist' and the more radical 'federalist' positions. While unionists promoted a limited and cautious form of European integration, based on intergovernmental principles and national sovereignty, federalists favoured supranational cooperation and the establishment of a constitution for a 'United States of Europe' (Dinan 1999). The main result of the European Movement was the birth of the Council of Europe in May

1949, which, in practice, implied the triumph of the unionist position.

Jean Monnet was an outsider and observer to the broadly based European Movement but he had come to realize during the Second World War that the formation of 'a federation or a European entity' among the states of Europe was the only means by which future conflict could be avoided (Monnet 1978, 222). For him, functional integration – close cooperation between countries in specific economic sectors – held the key to a future European federation and a prosperous Europe, devoid of its habitual conflict.

After studying the Convention of the Organization for European Economic Co-operation (OEEC), established in 1948 to administer the Marshall Plan for the reconstruction of Europe, a disappointed Monnet wrote to the French foreign affairs minister, George Bidault,

Efforts by the various countries, in the present national frameworks, will not in my view be enough. Furthermore, the idea that sixteen sovereign nations will co-operate effectively is an illusion. I believe that only the establishment of a *federation* of the West, including Britain, will enable us to solve our problems quickly enough, and finally prevent war. (Monnet 1978, 272)

The same message was repeated by Monnet to French prime minister Robert Schuman: 'The countries of Western Europe must turn their national efforts into a truly European effort. This will be possible only through a *federation* of the West' (1978, 272). Did this assertion emerge spontaneously from the non-bookish and practical Monnet, a man barely schooled, let alone schooled in the elevated and refined field of constitution-making? Probably not; it likely emerged from *his* school of higher education, through travelling. In Canada, he had observed the early successes of a so-called federation uniting different peoples and cultures. Yet the Canadian federation had begun as a confederation, an experiment that was probably the most that an unbridled optimist could hope for in a Europe bogged down in conflict for centuries. But then the Canadian confederation had developed over time into a federation and, more importantly, into an economically viable federation, a federation that Monnet, as a businessman, had seen could produce the goods.

The letters to Bidault and Schuman were written from Washington in April 1948. Monnet later admitted that he again felt inspired by the American temperament, or by the 'America on the move' attitude (Monnet 1978, 272). However, Monnet realized that it would be difficult to unite Europe into a federal entity because intensive and widespread nationalism and patriotism could not be easily displaced by the concept of 'Europe.' Nevertheless, Monnet believed that 'deeply entrenched habits of thought could be quickly modified in the pressure chambers of new institutions' (Ball 1982, 81). It might reasonably be expected that his observations and interactions with newly acculturated Old World European immigrants during his early travels in Canada shaped his confident optimism. He had been greatly impressed by the impact of new economic, cultural, and particularly political circumstances in conditioning people to new attitudes and ways of doing things to the benefit of all.

Be that as it may, the Allied decision to accept Germany again as a political entity and to assist in Germany's industrial reconstruction and revitalization, as bulwark against the post-war Soviet threat towards the end of the 1940s, made it evident that harsh and punitive French policies towards Germany had become outdated. The division of East from West Germany in 1949 made it absolutely imperative, in the words of Jean Monnet, 'that the time had come to act' (1978, 287). Monnet believed that the economic and security interests of France, as well as those of Europe, could be best stimulated and protected by a Franco-German reconciliation. George W. Ball, who worked closely with Monnet in 1949, and later became US ambassador to the United Nations and undersecretary of state in the Kennedy Administration, asserts unequivocally that Monnet fully realized that 'lasting peace could be achieved only by bringing France and Germany together and exorcising the demons of the past' (Ball 1982, 83).

French–German partnership was also the central ingredient in the proposal for a supranational coal and steel community, which Monnet sent to French prime minister Georges Bidault, and foreign affairs minister Robert Schuman, on 28 April 1950. At that point, Monnet knew that the Americans, on behalf of the Western occupying forces, had asked the French to outline a German policy at the foreign ministers' meeting in London on 11–13 May 1950. Monnet's proposal was quickly picked up by Schuman, who, coming from the disputed border region of Lorraine, realized that gathering together European nations required elimination of the old-age confrontation between France and Germany. In fact, Lorraine had changed hands between France and Germany in 1871, 1918, 1940, and 1945 (Dedman 1996), and Schuman, whose first language was German, did not become a French citizen until 1919.

The word *federation* was explicitly mentioned in Monnet's plan, which was officially presented as the Schuman Declaration on 9 May 1950:

By the pooling of basic production and the establishment of a new High Authority whose decisions will be binding on France, Germany, and the countries that join them, this proposal will lay the first concrete foundations of the *European Federation* which is indispensable to the maintenance of peace. (Emphasis added)[14]

It is apparent that Jean Monnet saw cooperation on basic natural resources and raw material – coal and steel – as a first step towards establishment of a political federation and 'the United States of Europe' (Monnet 1955). Coal and steel were of crucial importance to a nation-state's economic and military power, but for Monnet, the central idea was that France and Germany should share these resources in the service of peace. His background in the vineyards of Cognac may partly explain his focus on the resources supplied by nature as drivers of cooperation but so too can his early travels. Monnet witnessed first-hand the importance of natural resources and raw materials in the development of the Canadian confederation at the turn of the twentieth century. Moreover, he must have been told by his close friends in the Hudson's Bay Company that Canada had, in fact, emerged as a political entity with boundaries determined largely by the fur trade (Innis 1930).

The Treaty of Paris was signed on 18 April 1951, and the ECSC became a reality after the six founding members – Belgium, France, Germany, Italy, Luxembourg, and the Netherlands – completed ratification by the summer of 1952. Jean Monnet became president of the supranational High Authority of the ECSC, which started to function in 1953. From then on, Europeans from states that had spent years at war with each other proved capable of working and cooperating together, obeying common rules, and paying common taxes (Dedman 1996).

Although Jean Monnet's early trip to Canada kindled his optimism about political change, he realized that lasting change on the European political landscape had to be carefully organized (Monnet 1978, 46). The reference to Monnet as not only the practical technocrat but also as the 'EU's most original and important thinker' (Holland 1996, 101) is attributable, to a large extent, to his organizational skills. Monnet was a master of political design (Ugland 2009). In Duchêne's view (1991, 202), while most of the classic federations began by addressing traditional fields of state sovereignty, defence, and foreign policy, Monnet's proposed European federation was to be based on economic cooperation. This unique approach has been referred to as the 'Monnet method' of integration and it relied on trust and voluntary cooperation, rather than on power and compulsion. Monnet, as a theoretical innovator, provided the analytical link between what was often considered to be opposing doctrines: functionalism and federalism. From a functionalist perspective, political integration is seen as 'the gradual triumph of the rational and the technocratic over the political' (Pentland 1981, 551). Federalists, on the other hand, put politics at the forefront and promote an immediate shift of political power to the European level. Monnet's vision of a political federation was constructed on an incrementalist functionalistic logic. In his view, a political strategy of small, concrete, economic steps forging functional links among states would culminate in a federal Europe (Burgess 2009). In this sense he contributed to the 'federalization of functionalism,' a concept developed by Navari (1996, 72).

Conclusion

In sum, Jean Monnet's early encounters with Canada and Canadians served as muses for his lifelong work on European supranational unity. It would certainly be an exaggeration to state that Monnet imprinted his exceptional political mark on Europe as a result of his voyage to Canada as a teenager. However, despite the substantial time lag, Monnet's ideas for Europe were clearly prompted by the contrasts between the Old and the New World, which he, for the first time, discovered in Canada in 1907. The social and political insights from this trip deeply influenced him when in 1950 he presented his plan for supranational European unity.

Yet it must be emphasized that Monnet's trip was not motivated by analytical or theoretical considerations. Nevertheless, he should be considered a more significant theoretical figure than he has been. Monnet relied on a method of comparison and sought to draw lessons from the similarities and differences he observed. In this sense, Monnet worked as a theorist. It can, of course, be argued that Monnet provided only a very selective picture of life in Canada through his empirical observations. However, such is often the case, because theorists give us 'pictures of political life in miniature, pictures in which what is extraneous to the theorist's purpose has been deleted' (Wolin 2004, 19). They do so to construct models in order to render political phenomena intellectually manageable. Monnet always emphasized the general view – *vue générale* – in his work for European supranational unity (Fontaine 1991b), while details often stood in the background (Ugland 2009).

Complex details – the seemingly minor events in life – were often transformed to general views while Monnet was walking: 'To see it clearly I have to concentrate – which I can do only in isolation, on long solitary walks' (Monnet 1978, 288). Monnet claimed that his habitual taste for long walks was first acquired in the Canadian Rockies (46). He began each day with breakfast at 7 o'clock followed by an hour's walk. Subsequently, he made every effort to spend a fortnight, twice yearly, in the remote mountains of the Alps with a rucksack on his back in the company of his long-time favourite guide. This was Monnet's form of relaxation and recreation, but it was also a practice and tool employed before he made major decisions. It was after a two-week trip to the Swiss Alps, hiking from lodge to lodge in the spring of 1950, that Monnet presented his general view for a European Coal and Steel Community, a proposal that had far-reaching consequences for the future of Europe. Evidently, there were other details in other frames that contributed to his general views. His relationship with the Hudson's Bay Company, which we explore next, is one of the most significant.

3

Monnet and the Hudson's Bay Company

On my travels I had learned that economic forces were not blind and abstract, but could be measured and steered. Above all, I had come to realize that where there was organization there was real strength.

Jean Monnet (1978, 49)

Economic forces had been 'measured and steered' in Canada for four decades by the time Jean Monnet arrived in 1907. The very creation of the dominion had been intended to control pressing economic factors and to address the exigencies of defence – factors that have been described elsewhere in compelling detail (see, for instance, Cook 1986; Creighton 1970; Smiley 1978).

Renowned Canadian historian Edgar McInnis (1969) indicates that the debates among Canada's founding fathers of Confederation were peppered with references to the history and literature of American constitutional development. That may be so, but the outcome of their deliberations, the British North America Act, 1867, certainly did not reflect the lofty philosophical concerns for rights and freedoms embedded in its American counterpart. Quite the contrary, the Canadian document was very much like a commercial contract, even containing a now 'repealed clause' (section 145) requiring the dominion government to commence the building of an intercolonial railroad within six months after the union to connect Halifax with the St Lawrence River (see Van Loon and Whittington 1987, 685).

With organization, there is undoubtedly 'real strength,' because section 145 was satisfied in record time and, despite the enormity of the geo-physical obstacles, a railroad from sea to sea was completed by the mid-1880s. Moreover, it seems that the final strength in organization with primarily economic goals, and one devoid of the emotive nationalist sentiment burgeoning in Europe prior to the First World War, was its obvious ability to lay the infrastructure for the wave of prosperity that met Monnet on his arrival. It was apparent that by the turn of the twentieth century there were great rewards to be reaped from Canada's four-decade-old model of growth so eloquently described by McInnis as a 'slow and tenacious advance from one step to another along the road to nationhood, the patient evolution of successive compromises in politics and government, the determined conquest of the physical obstacles to national economic development' (1969, vii).

Patience and compromise, according to McInnis (1969, vii), were 'virtues born of necessity,' just as economic unions and inventions are. It is unlikely that Monnet was well acquainted with the Dominion of Canada's short history and its endemic virtues. However, he was an astute individual, one of those rare types who, blessed with an excess of common sense, could distil 'the blind and abstract' essentials of a good deal into tangible ingredients to mix with his next deal. But the blind and abstract were staring him in the face. How could he not discern or be imbued or even buttressed with the virtues of patience and compromise during his travels to Canada? Canada's economic union had grown from four provinces to nine, with the two most recent additions, Saskatchewan and Alberta, being carved from the Northwest Territories just two years before he laid foot on Canadian soil. Indeed, patience and compromise were the quintessential building blocks of Europe's initial ECSC contract among six states, to an EC, and upwards to an EU with twenty-seven members – an expansion strikingly similar to Canada's early expansion.

But then let us assume for the sake of the argument a tenuous connection between Canada's development experience, in all of its limitless potential in the early twentieth century, and Monnet's perception of its vital driving forces. Then surely he would have ascertained the value of these virtues from his successful involvement with the venerable Hudson's Bay Company (HBC). Compromise and patience were compulsory if one were to come to terms with the HBC because of its bifurcated executive, which straddled the Atlantic.

The HBC was a legendary company that Monnet certainly recognized as an organization of 'real strength.' It was a seventeenth-century invention: the mammoth joint stock trading company that launched the modern era of globalization. Timothy Brook, with metaphoric flair, describes the first such venture, created in 1602: 'The Dutch East India – the VOC, as it is known – is to corporate capitalism what Benjamin Franklin's kite is to electronics' (Brook 2008, 15). But we know that lightning never strikes twice in the same place. It struck again in Britain when in 1670 King Charles II granted a charter to the 'The Governor and Company of Adventurers of England Trading into Hudson's Bay.' Under the terms of its charter, the company was granted

the sole trade and commerce of all these seas, straits, bays, rivers, lakes, creeks, and sounds, in whatsoever latitude they shall be, that lie within the entrance of the straits, commonly called Hudson's Straits, together with all the lands and territories upon the countries, coasts and confines of the seas, bays, lakes, rivers, creeks and sounds aforesaid. (Burpee 1948, 212)

This land was referred to as Rupert's Land after the name of the first governor of the HBC, Prince Rupert of the Rhine, who was the nephew of King Charles I of England. The actual boundaries of Rupert's Land were not clearly defined, but the generally accepted view has been that they included all territory draining into Hudson Bay, from Labrador to the Rocky Mountains and from Chester-field Inlet in Nunavut to the source of the Red River in the United States (Burpee 1948). In 1869, Rupert's Land was sold through a cash settlement to the new nation of Canada by the Hudson's Bay Company. In fact, Canada emerged as a political entity with boundaries determined largely by the fur trade, the primary pursuit of the HBC (Innis 1930). While London was the principal market for the fur pelts, a wide variety of goods were exported from England in return. Alcoholic beverages were among those goods, and in his memoirs Monnet referred directly to the significant role alcohol played in the lucrative fur trade: 'We needed furs: the trappers liked cognac' (Monnet 1978, 46). However, things are never as simple as they seem.

Selling Alcohol in Canada

Commercial transactions are rarely tidy, mainly because there is more to them than the clarity of thought presented by neat numbers, black or red. Human beings with their jumble of diverse interests and emotions are also involved. The HBC was no exception. Peter C. Newman's memorable three volumes on the history of the HBC indicate that in the aftermath of the sale of Rupert's Land to Canada and the concomitant transition of HBC men from 'merchant adventurers to merchant princes,' the company's senior management became embroiled in classic internecine warfare with 'governors, deputy governors and their ennobled retinues trying to *rule* the Company from London pitted against a group of fiercely proud, down-home Good Old Boys trying to *run* the Company from Winnipeg' (Newman 1991, 257).

As a neophyte supplicant to the Winnipeg Good Old Boys of the HBC in 1907, Monnet probably would have been unaware of the struggles between factions in the top brass of the company, who, according to Newman, battled with 'the

obdurate conviction of crusaders' (1991, 257). Nevertheless, in his transatlantic connections with the rival parties,
Monnet would have been required to serve an apprenticeship in compromise and patience. And he did so successfully as he overcame Old World–New World antagonism, as
the following pages acknowledge.

More to the point, the value of his successful apprenticeship was eventually recognized in a grander project – the
ECSC – requiring deep-seated skills of compromise and
patience that, if combined with McInnis's third virtue – tenacity – would amount to *leadership* in today's parlance. One
had to be exceedingly tenacious – and overly optimistic – to
expect to sell cognac in Canada in the early years of the
twentieth century.

The sale and distribution of alcoholic beverages was
more than just a contentious issue in Canada. It had been
a constitutional issue. During the last two decades of the
nineteenth century, the legislative powers of the federal
and provincial governments were determined largely on
the basis of judgments relating to the sale of 'intoxicating
liquors,' which in one early case was likened to a 'disease'
affecting 'public morals' and endangering 'public safety'
(see Russell v. The Queen, in Russell, Knopff, and Morton
1989, 46–7).

The Canadian temperance movement, which began in
the 1820s, was a popular movement with significant influence at the time of Monnet's first long voyage (Smart and
Ogborne 1996). Its message was clear and to the point: the
consumption of intoxicating beverages was the root of all
evil, and more particularly, the root of social dislocation.
Abstinence as personal solution, and prohibition as public
policy remedy, were the key objectives of the movement.
Both received widespread acceptance. Many of the devoted
and of the converts 'signed the pledge' to abstain, while
prohibition became increasingly fashionable. For instance,
just nine years before Monnet landed in Canada, the temperance movement had successfully lobbied the dominion

government to hold a national referendum on prohibition. Then on 29 September 1898, Canadians were asked to vote on whether they were 'in favour of passing an act prohibiting the importation, manufacture, or sale of spirits, wine, ale, cider and all other alcoholic liquors for use as a beverage?' Out of the 543,029 votes cast nationally, 52.5 per cent voted in favour. Furthermore, majority support for prohibition was secured in all provinces except Quebec (Smart and Ogborne 1996).

Nevertheless, Prime Minister Sir Wilfrid Laurier chose to disregard the voice of the Canadian people. He argued that because turnout was low (44 per cent), 'the expression of public opinion recorded at the polls in favour of Prohibition did not justify the introduction by the Government of a prohibitory measure' (Smart and Ogborne 1996, 46). Subsequent to the failure of the national referendum, the temperance movement turned its attention to having prohibition introduced in the provinces. Its strategy succeeded only in Prince Edward Island. Accordingly, J.G. Monnet & Co. Cognac would have received an ambivalent reception in all other provinces upon his arrival in 1907. But then, even they introduced some kind of temporary prohibition in connection with the First World War in order to ensure that grain and fruits were used for food instead of for alcoholic beverages.[15]

Monnet never alluded to confrontations with the temperance movement, if indeed there were any, but it is well known that the 'liquor interests' – of which Jean Monnet was a representative – were singled out as the movement's public enemy number one. In a well-known Canadian temperance song 'Away with the Wine' from 1874, the message is clear:

Free the land that we love from the dramseller's blight,
From the demon that dwells in the wine.
Away then, away with the wine.
Away then, away with the wine. (Coates and Brothers 1874, 50)

Amazingly, Jean Monnet set out to search for new markets and to expand the relationship between his father's cognac company and the HBC in an atmosphere of substantial hostility – either a litmus test or a perfecting of his tenacity, or more probably both. At any rate, the earliest reference to the relationship between J.G. Monnet & Co. Cognac and the HBC dates back to 5 January 1896.[16] So the groundwork for Monnet's expedition must have begun a decade in advance. Hence, the eighteen-year-old Monnet was well positioned to conduct 'extensive business' with the HBC and to develop contacts with leading figures in the company (Monnet 1978, 46). For instance, Monnet mentions that he was invited to Fort Selkirk in the distant Yukon by Mr Chapman, the chairman of the HBC, which would have been a most exceptional invitation for a youngster without prior connections to the HBC. Also, Monnet developed a close relationship with the London-based governor of the Hudson's Bay Company, Robert Kindersley, and the deputy governor, Charles Sale.[17] As it turned out, Kindersley and Sale played key roles in Monnet's endeavours to uphold Allied supply lines during the First World War, but more on that later.

Vibrant Winnipeg was Monnet's ostensible *terminus ad quem* because it was the Canadian headquarters for the HBC. It was also the mid-continent distribution point between the East and West – an aspiring Canadian Chicago. Yet he travelled across Canada and visited many destinations between 1907 and 1914. The year 1910 seems to have been particularly hectic for Monnet because he visited a seemingly endless list of customers from Montreal to Vancouver. He admitted that 'this took a lot of patience and hard work' (Monnet 1978, 46). Thus, patience and tenacity were being groomed, with 'compromise' yet to be refined – qualities that would serve him well in the European unification project.

Monnet's notes and new orders, resulting from these meetings with customers, were communicated to Cognac at regular intervals.[18] The linkages between the New and the

Old World were also kept alive through his travelling. During this period and between his travels in Canada, Monnet spent much time at the main headquarters of the HBC in London, England.[19] He also returned frequently to Cognac to meet with the producers of Cognac. In his memoirs, Monnet refers to a visit with M. Barrault, a supplier of the raw eau de vie for J.G. Monnet & Co., in the village of Segonzac near Cognac:

M. Barrault was in the vineyard, and I found him driving his own cart, dressed in an old tail-coat. Canada, its forests, its snows and its trappers, seemed to belong to another world. But it was this other world that M. Barrault wanted to know about. Even before I could ask him about the harvest, he said: 'Well, what's the news from Winnipeg?' (Monnet 1978, 45)

As wide ranging as his friendly discussions of Canada may have been, his conversations about France tended to focus on cognac. Monnet's principal message to Canadians was that his father's cognac was 'as reputable as the best-known brands, and that it was cheaper' (Monnet 1978, 46). His persistence was remunerated handsomely. In 1911, he negotiated a five-year agreement in which J.G. Monnet & Co. became the sole supplier of brandy to the HBC throughout the Canadian West from Fort William (at the western end of Lake Superior in Ontario) to Vancouver Island.[20] The contract was drafted by Jean Monnet in Winnipeg on 15 September 1911, and it was based on conversations and negotiations between Monnet and the HBC's Herbert Burbidge, the son of renowned retailer Richard Burbidge.[21]

According to the contract, the HBC agreed to not serve as an agent for other brandies, except for Martell or Hennessy in British Columbia. It is also stated that the HBC was committed to 'use its best endeavors to promoting the sale' of the J.G. Monnet & Co. brandies. This contract made the HBC one of the largest clients of J.G. Monnet & Co. Cognac in the world. In return, the HBC was to earn a commission of 12 per cent on all sales. The commission would be deducted from the payment of every invoice. In addition, the HBC was entitled to one complimentary case of brandy for every twenty ordered during the first year of the agreement.

Monnet corresponded with his father throughout the negotiations. The letters show deep affection and respect between the two and they reveal that the young Monnet relied heavily on his father's business acumen, which is precisely why the letters are filled with questions by the younger Monnet on how to proceed.[22] The elder Monnet made no effort whatsoever to conceal his adulation and pride for his son, and his full confidence in him when, upon sealing the deal, he wrote to an HBC official that the arrangement would be facilitated by the 'help of the effort of a special man, whom we will send out during the Spring of next year.'[23] He then added, 'We expect that our Mr Jean Monnet himself will take this journey and we feel convinced that his effort will be mutually beneficial.'[24]

The contract was confirmed by HBC's Burbidge in a letter addressed to Monnet, dated 18 September 1911:

Dear Sir, I have to acknowledge receipt of your letter of the 15th inst. offering to the Hudson's Bay Company the agency for United Vineyard Proprietors' Company's Brandies in Western Canada, from Fort William, to the Pacific Coast, and I write to inform you that the terms outlined therein are agreeable to us, and I am arranging to have the agreement drawn up and ratified in London.

I trust this agency will result in mutual advantage both to your firm and the Hudson's Bay Company, and in order to accomplish this I wish to assure you of our best efforts to make a success of the Agency.[25]

This initial contract represented the beginning of an extensive and prolonged trading relationship between the United Vineyard Proprietors Company of Cognac and the

Hudson's Bay Company, and the agreement between the two companies was renewed several times.

But all was not wine and roses for Monnet in this period. His apprenticeship in patience, compromise, and tenacity was put to severe tests, one of which was the harsh environment in which he found himself. Jean Monnet was captivated by the pioneer life in the New World. However, later he admitted that the climate in the new towns along the Canadian Pacific Railway, where men often outnumbered women several times over, was tough. For instance, in 1911, adult males (twenty-one years and over) outnumbered females 184.3 to 100 in Alberta, 137.7 to 100 in Manitoba, and 181.2 to 100 in Saskatchewan.[26] Of Calgary's 43,704 inhabitants in 1911, 26,565 were men and 17,139 women.[27] The gender imbalance engendered a number of social problems, such as alcohol abuse and prostitution. Despite his business, or perhaps because of his business, Monnet was not much of a drinker. Yet he confessed that the saloon was his only comfort at times during his early years in Canada, and disclosed that once – the only time in his life – he actually became genuinely drunk in one of the local watering holes (Roussel 1996, 35). It may have been of little comfort to him, but Monnet was not alone in this regard. This period can best be described as a 'wet' one by Canadian standards, and it was accompanied with increasing alcohol-related problems. For instance, convictions for alcohol-related offences – like drunkenness and offences under the Liquor Control Acts – doubled between 1907 and 1914 (Popham and Schmidt 1958). In fact, it took more than four decades – until 1946 with 63,953 offences – and with major increases in population, for the Canada-wide number of offences for drunkenness to surpass the 1913 record of 60,915.

Of course none of this was lost on the stalwarts of temperance. Temperance songs of the period aptly capture their mood (Smart and Ogborne 1996). The Ontario evangelist John M. Whyte with his song 'Oh the Drinking!' from 1898 provides a striking illustration of the atmosphere:

Oh the drinking, sinful drinking,
Glasses ring and voices cheer,
While to drunkards' graves are sinking
Half a million every year. (Whyte 1981, 1)[28]

Another source of strain on Monnet was the grim financial situation of his father's company, which struggled,
together with many other smaller companies involved
in the alcohol industry, to make ends meet in the period
leading up to the First World War. Around 1910, cognac
inventories accumulated and, in accordance with the laws
of supply and demand, revenues plunged. In 1911, stock
options raised sufficient capital to enable the company to
ride this difficult patch, but the relief was short-lived. The
year 1913 seemed to be almost calamitous, as the inventories began to accumulate again and debt burgeoned. The
financial situation in 1913 was so critical that a representative for the company hesitated to send a telegram to Jean
Monnet in Canada because of the cost associated with this
correspondence! It is in this context that Jean Monnet was
asked to sell more abroad, but also to rationalize the way
the company did business (Roussel 1996).

As if matters were not bad enough, Monnet's health took
a turn for the worse. In April 1913, while staying in Winnipeg, Monnet was struck with acute appendicitis.[29] At that
time, mortality and morbidity rates from acute appendicitis
remained high, and Monnet's parents – particularly his
mother, Maria Demelle Monnet – back at home in Cognac
were very concerned for their son's health.[30] An employee
of his father's company was dispatched to send a telegram to
Monnet urging him to return home to France for an operation.[31] Monnet ignored the advice and had his appendix
removed in North America. He seemed to have recovered
from the operation by 15 May (Roussel 1996).

It is likely that Monnet's surgery was conducted at the General Hospital in Winnipeg. The hospital attracted patients
from communities along the Canadian Pacific Railway line

from Port Arthur, Ontario, in the east, to Calgary in the west (Gagan and Gagan 2002). The hospital experienced a tremendous growth in keeping with the city's expanding population. For instance, annual admissions to the hospital increased 234 per cent between 1900 and 1914, and surgical admissions by 327 per cent (Gagan and Gagan 2002). Monnet also came down with typhoid fever during his time in Canada but he apparently also recovered relatively quickly from what was then a potentially deadly bacterial infection. In fact, typhoid was among the leading causes of death among Canadians between the ages of fifteen and fifty during the period.

Jean Monnet was in good health when he returned from Canada to France via London in 1914 just before the outbreak of the First World War. In fact, he learned the unfortunate news that France was mobilizing for war at the Poitiers train station. Monnet had been found medically unfit for military service in 1904, following a medical examination that revealed lung problems. Accordingly, he decided to serve the Allied cause in other ways. It was evident to him that the Allies had to coordinate their war efforts. Specifically, Monnet was convinced that France and Great Britain had to work together. So once again Necessity entered Monnet's picture when, back home in Cognac, the twenty-five-year-old Jean Monnet discovered a window of opportunity to transmit to political elites his message of the need for joint Allied action:

One of our friends at Cognac was a lawyer, Maître Fernand Benon, who happened to know René Viviani, the Prime Minister, quite well: he had appeared with him in several court cases. He was open to new ideas. He asked me questions about my travels, and I in turn asked him about the affairs in France. (Monnet 1978, 50)

According to Monnet, he had no difficulty persuading Benon about the veracity of his misgivings on the apparent lack of cooperation among the Allies. Benon, in turn, agreed to introduce Monnet to Prime Minister Viviani. In his memoirs, Monnet claims that his own family thought he was 'big-headed to want to by-pass everyone and go straight to the top' and to think that he had something worthwhile to convey to the prime minister (Monnet 1978, 50). According to Monnet, he was daring because he knew no taboos and was unaware of the importance of official functions: 'Like Americans, I was trained to think if something needs to be changed every man has the right to point this out' (Bromberger and Bromberger 1969, 13).

At an early stage during the war, it became clear to Monnet that the French merchant marine would be unable to transport the colossal amount of supplies required to continue the war and that the country would be dependent upon foreign shipping. Monnet met with Prime Minister Viviani in September 1914. Monnet claims that he did not present an elaborated proposal to the prime minister, but that he had 'a conviction to express' (Monnet 1978, 51). He told the prime minister that France and Great Britain should not compete with each other, but instead 'set up joint bodies to estimate the combined resources of the Allies, share them out, and share the posts ... Allied solidarity must be total' (51–2).

Prime Minister Viviani, whose two sons had recently died in the Battle of the Marne, must have been convinced by the ideas and arguments outlined by the young man, and in November 1914 Monnet was sent to London to work for the French Civil Supplies Service. The prime minister thought Monnet was the right man for the job, not just because of the nearly flawless English that he had perfected in Canada, but also because of his creative mind, a mind that was more common among North American businessmen than among traditional French officials. According to Georges Berthoin, who served as principal private secretary to Jean Monnet when he was president of the High Authority of the ECSC, his North American direct work methods marked him: 'The American is on the same footing with everyone, and Monnet was like that, which made him singular with respect to European ways of thinking. Thus he became a Frenchman somewhat different from the others' (Roussel 1996, 131; my translation).[32] Significantly, Monnet relied directly on the experiences and the people he had encountered in Canada in his new job in London. It seems that one tends to gravitate to those who are like-minded.

Negotiating Supplies for Europe with the Hudson's Bay Company during the First World War

In London, Jean Monnet realized early on the chaotic nature of the supply effort for the war. In order to bring about order and cooperation, Monnet relied on the friendly relations he had developed with the Hudson's Bay Company during his first trip to Canada. According to Governor Robert Kindersley and Deputy Governor Charles Sale of the HBC, by August 1914 Monnet had already proposed that the Hudson's Bay Company become the French government's purchasing agent for vital civilian supplies, such as foodstuffs, raw materials, and manufactured goods.[33]

The first contract between the HBC and the French government was signed on 9 October 1914, with Jean Monnet and the HBC secretary, Frank Ingrams, as chief negotiators. Under the terms of the agreement, the HBC was responsible for arranging credit for all purchases on behalf of the French government and for organizing shipping to transport the goods to French ports.

In due course, the HBC signed approximately 6,600 separate contracts with various agencies of the French government. Additional agreements were also later signed with the governments of Belgium, Romania, and Russia. In carrying out these contracts, the HBC engaged 145 agencies in countries around the world, with the largest ones in Liverpool, Montreal, New York, and Archangel on the northeastern tip of Russia. While the HBC had long experience in buying and shipping goods, the company's small fleets could

Jean Monnet, the father of Europe.
(Copyright: The European Commission)

R.M.S. Virginian. (Allan Line) 12 000 Tons, Turbine

Jean Monnet's first trip to Canada occurred in 1907. He arrived in Montreal via Quebec City from Liverpool aboard the SS *Virginian*. (Norwegian Heritage)

Jean Monnet was sent to Canada to promote his father's cognac company. (Photo: Pierre Guerette)

Royal Alexandra C. P. R. Hotel, Winnipeg, Can.

Postcards from the Royal Alexandra Hotel in Winnipeg, 1907. (Courtesy of the author)

ROTUNDA, ROYAL ALEXANDRA HOTEL

Jean Monnet at Niagara Falls, 1907. (Copyright: Zybach & Co.
Source: Fondation Jean Monnet pour l'Europe, Lausanne,
Switzerland)

Previously unpublished photograph of Monnet at an outdoor
restaurant in Montreal, 1913. (Source: Fondation Jean Monnet
pour l'Europe, Lausanne, Switzerland)

Many countries have honoured the memory of Jean Monnet with stamps – Belgium, France, Germany, Luxembourg, Monaco, Portugal, Republic of Guinea, and Spain. Perhaps Canada will one day join the list.

(Courtesy of the author)

be counted on the fingers of one hand. In order to ensure the transport of supplies to French ports, the Bay Steam Ship Company, a subsidiary, was set up and a merchant fleet consisting of several hundred ships was created. Over 13 million tons of goods were transported, representing a turnover of £150 million, on which the HBC charged a 1 per cent commission (Schooling 1920). Despite the loss of 110 vessels, mostly destroyed by German U-boats, all parties considered the organization for supplying the Allies a success. All in all, the HBC provided a notable link in the supply chains that helped the Allies win the First World War (Duchêne 1994, 34), and Jean Monnet played a key role in initiating, establishing, and maintaining the link.

Monnet devotes little attention to these noteworthy events in his memoirs, and Duchêne finds the omission intriguing: 'There seems to be nothing to blush about in having initiated, or helped to initiate, a useful connection that lasted until 1922 and was a precursor of similar deals' (1994, 34). Duchêne speculates on several explanations. First, Monnet in his memoirs seemed more interested in the political aspects of his life than in its business aspects. Second, because of the strong reliance on the British-owned HBC, there was also ill-feeling about the arrangement in the French civil service. Perhaps Monnet did not want to remind his public about his exceedingly cosy British connections some fifty years later. Third, although Monnet made a point of not taking any commission from the HBC, he may have been fearful of being accused of using his HBC connections for private gain. For instance, it is true that the HBC lent him £40,000 in 1922, when his family's company faced severe economic difficulties and most likely saved J.G. Monnet & Co. from bankruptcy. Monnet always seemed to be a 'healthy puritan' about separating public service from private gain, so there seems to have been nothing untoward in the transaction (Duchêne 1994, 34). However, François Fontaine, who assisted Monnet in writing his memoirs, may have the most plausible explanation. According to Fon-

taine, Monnet was uninterested in figures or legal texts,
and he did not keep a detailed journal about his activities:
'His Memoirs owe very little to his memory, which registered actual events badly. He only retained their essence'
(Fontaine 1991a, 20). For Monnet, the main point was that
the Allies joined in the war effort, and that the HBC was a
catalyst at his behest.

Both the extraordinary friendship between Jean Monnet
and the HBC and Monnet's self-sacrifice are clearly divulged
in a report to the HBC Board justifying the £40,000 loan.
The report dated 28 March 1922 and signed by the deputy
governor, Charles Sale, is worth quoting in its entirety:

In August 1914 Jean Monnet, a member of a firm with whom the
Company have done business for over [blank] years, suggested
that the Company should become purchasing agents for the
French Government. The fact that we received that appointment
was due entirely to his initiative and efforts. The unique arrangements for Finance, whereby the Company had and still have a
blank credit on the French Treasury was made by him in 1915,
and in many other ways and on many other occasions Monnet's
actions and influences were essential to the safety and success of
operations.

Monnet's influences throughout the War lay partly in the fact
that he was not a member of the French Civil Services. He never
asked us for a commission nor have we ever paid anything. He
insisted upon paying his own expenses whether in this country or
in France or in travelling, even when such expenses were solely
incurred in connection with the transactions between the French
Government and ourselves. This situation has left the company
under a very considerable obligation to Mr Monnet, especially as
the Hudson's Bay Company has made from the French business,
very large profits totalling over one million pounds, a great part
of this profit accruing since the war. He entirely neglected his
own personal interests, both during and after the War, leaving
them in hands of others.

Unfortunately during the last two years the Cognac, in which

Monnet's interests solely lie, has, in common with other parts of the world, been passing through a series of crises and Mr Monnet has suffered considerable financial losses. Mr Monnet realises that he must give up his National work as soon as possible in order to repair his sources of income, and for this purpose he must have some financial assistance.

The Governor [Kindersley] and I feel that the time has arrived, before finally closing the French accounts, when Mr Monnet's services should receive recognition from the Company.

In talking over affairs with Monnet we find that he rejects entirely any suggestion of obligation on the part of the Company to recoup him for his share in the operation by payment of a Commission, but both the Governor and myself feel that the obligation does exist and that the Company, even if we consider only the period since the Armistice, having made good profits out of the association should requite Monnet in some way or another. The suggestion now is that the Company should advance £40,000 at a reasonable interest on such security whether sufficient to cover this amount or not, as Monnet may desire to offer or be in a position to give.

Both the Governor and myself think it likely that the amount will be repaid in full, but in making the recommendation wish it to be understood that it might not be recoverable. In view however of the undoubted obligation to Monnet we think the risk should be taken.[34]

This recommendation was unanimously agreed to by the Board. Monnet repaid the loan with interest in 1930.[35]

Conclusion

Patience, compromise, and tenacity have been identified as key virtues, embedded in the curriculum of Monnet's Canadian School of Experience. His exceptional political mark on Europe would not have been etched without them. Monnet truly valued patience and saw it as a necessary ingredient in everything from brandy production to the unification of states and people. He could be persistent on what he thought was essential but he was also pragmatic. His approach to political integration was, for instance, always a compromise between long-term ideals and immediate political realities. He said in his memoirs, 'Once I have reached a conclusion that I want others to share, I am never afraid to repeat myself' (Monnet 1978, 126). In this respect, he often compared himself to his maternal grandmother, who used to be known as 'Marie la Rabâcheuse.' However, his renowned tenacity is best defined by his friend George W. Ball: 'Monnet's life confirms the old saying that a deeply committed man can move mountains. Yet to do so he must, like Monnet, possess indefatigable energy, an uncommon measure of both resilience and resourcefulness, and the willingness to forgo all personal gain and glory in the single-minded pursuit of a transcendent purpose' (1982, 95–6).

Canada served Monnet as well as Monnet served Canada. Patience, compromise, and tenacity, as was indicated at the beginning of this chapter, can be encapsulated in one word: *leadership*. And leadership can lead to statesmanship. To be sure, Monnet became skilled in the essentials of both in Canada and put them to immediate use – or more likely to the immediate test – with the outbreak of the First World War. His skills were justifiably recognized and employed to bring to fruition a better world. Largely on the basis of his impressive achievements in both London and Paris, Monnet was appointed deputy secretary-general of the League of Nations under Sir Eric Drummond in 1919. In Geneva, he made a substantial contribution to achieving a temporary solution to two problems: the settlement of the German-Polish disputes over Upper Silesia, and the restoration of Austrian finances, involving a loan of $130 million by the great powers.

Monnet resigned from the League of Nations in December 1922 in order to return to Cognac to save the family company J.G. Monnet & Co. Cognac. The consumption of cognac fell during the First World War and its aftermath, and, as might be expected, prices plummeted. Wartime prohibition in Canada and then prohibition in the United States certainly reduced demand and profits. Between 1923 and 1925, Monnet reorganized the family company, paid its debts, and made it profitable again. He would have been helped, of course, by the repeal of prohibition in most Canadian provinces by 1925 and eventually by the termination of the United States' 'Noble Experiment' in 1933.

Monnet's encounters with Canada and Canadians played an important role in his early successes, and they have been identified as lessons that conditioned his meditative and collaborative style that could obviate the potential destructiveness of national borders and cultures (Hermann 1968, 6–7; Roussel 1996). He continued to look to Canada as inspiration for creative solutions throughout his long career. The next chapter demonstrates as much, as we present his role in another tragic scene: the preparation for the Second World War.

4

Monnet's Canadian Scheme in Preparation for the Second World War

Everywhere I had the same impression: that where physical space was unlimited, confidence was unlimited too. Where change was accepted, expansion was assured. The United States had retained the dynamism of the Western pioneers, like those I had seen in action in Winnipeg. But to that they had added organization. To organize change – that, I saw, was necessary, and it could be done.

Jean Monnet (1978, 46)

To the early-twenty-first-century mind, the notion that change requires organization must seem obvious but the notion was not so evident a hundred years ago. Organizational theory was in its heyday, with both academic and practical thinkers identifying new organizational principles and practices that would eventually be absorbed into the structures of large-scale enterprises, both private and public, and into procedures and processes. The impact of classical organization theorists was substantial enough to convince management gurus, like Peter Drucker, to hail their achievements as culminating in a 'productivity revolution,' a putative 'revolution' that continues to this day (Drucker 1994, 32–3). Drucker, referring to one of the single most important – and controversial – figures of classical organizational theory, Frederick W. Taylor, makes a somewhat hyperbolic claim: '"Darwin, Marx, Freud" form the trinity often cited as the "makers of the modern world." Marx would be taken out and replaced by Taylor if there were any justice in the world. But that Taylor is not given his due is a minor matter' (Drucker 1994, 39). The major matter and Drucker's major point is that Taylor was substantially responsible for triggering the productivity explosion of the last century. Industrialization and its concomitant prosperity would not have progressed as it did without organization, and particularly without new organizational models.

More to the point, momentous thoughts that change our ways have a way of seeping into conventional thought. How could it be otherwise? New fashions make headlines and then become mainstream vogue. For example, Frederick W. Taylor's 'principles of scientific management' were deemed to be of such importance that he was called to appear before the US Special Committee of the House of Representatives to investigate Taylor and Other Systems of Shop Management in 1912 (Taylor 1911). Taylor appeared before the Special Committee only a year before Henry Ford introduced moving assembly belts – a concept borrowed from meat packers in Chicago – to his plant in Detroit, and introducing the world to 'Fordism,' for better or for worse.

Monnet may or may not have been aware of the newly articulated praxis of meshing means to ends by way of thinking about organizations. But the new organizational structures and processes would certainly have leaked into his *theoria*, conditioned, as it would have been, not just by travel, but also by experience and by vogue – and especially by vogue related to business affairs. As Drucker puts it, new organizational paradigms 'swept' through countries at different times (Drucker 1999, 139) but they did indeed sweep through the Western world, affecting those involved in weighty affairs of high business and of state.[36] Monnet would have been affected by the sweeps because his generation learned in much the same way contemporary organizational theorists of the day arrived at their conclusions: it was an applied science where they learned by doing and by taking clues and cues for doing things better wherever they could find them. But they usually found them in business and then imported them to the affairs of state. Business is where Monnet acquired his appreciation for organization and where he honed his organizational skills in the interwar years, after a brief stint in the League of Nations. Then, like a Canadian 'C.D. Howe boy,' he was drawn to government when the Second World War began, ending a tumultuous career in international finance, the story of which is compelling in itself.[37]

Monnet and International Finance

After his resignation from the League of Nations and a short period back in Cognac to resuscitate his flagging family company, Monnet was, in 1926, approached by the American investment bank Blair and Co. to set up a European branch in Paris. Blair and Co. was well known for having negotiated loans during the First World War for countries allied to the United States. Blair discovered Monnet's leadership and organizational talents when the company negotiated loans for the government of France. Monnet was the vice-president and managing partner of European Blair until 1929, where he successfully negotiated major loans to Poland and Romania. According to Duchêne (1994), Monnet's affiliation with Blair enabled him to further expand his extensive network of contacts – a highly important asset as he segued from business leader to full statesman. Expansion of his network of important connections began almost immediately on his entry to the field of high finance. In connection with the negotiations for the Polish loan, Monnet met up again with John Foster Dulles, whom he had first met at the Paris Peace Conference, when Dulles was a lawyer on the American delegation. Monnet developed a close friendship with Dulles, who later became President Eisenhower's secretary of state (1953–9) and prominent Cold War warrior.[38] Dulles' web of contacts, among others, would have certainly been useful to Monnet in establishing a reputation as a man who could always find the right people to do things.

In the spring of 1929, Blair & Co. transferred its assets to Transamerica, a newly created holding company, located in San Francisco, on which Monnet served as vice-chairman. However, the Wall Street Crash in October 1929 hit the overextended Transamerica, whose shares plunged from a high of $165 in 1929 to a breathtaking low of $2 by 1931 (Duchêne 1994, 48). Monnet seemed to take his brief but financially catastrophic time with Transamerica in stride: 'In San Francisco, I made and then lost a great deal of money. Experience was all I added to my capital. At forty, I was still learning – indeed, I have never stopped' (Monnet 1978, 109). He once told the American statesman and close friend George W. Ball that he lost five million dollars (Ball 1982).[39]

All in all, the Transamerica project clearly cost Monnet a fortune and according to Duchêne he never acquired another: 'In fact, from 1932 to the end of his life, though he always seems to have spent fairly freely, he was equally never quite on an even financial keel' (1994, 49). According to an interview with Monnet in *Fortune* magazine in 1944, 'salary-wise [Monnet] has from time to time earned good money. Capital-wise he has accumulated very little' (Davenport 1944, 124). Despite such private setbacks, Monnet was always able to count on his well-off friends in high places to help boost his financial viability again. John Foster Dulles, and Sir Robert Kindersley – at the Lazard Brothers and former governor of the Hudson's Bay Company – were always most ready and willing to assist him.

After the 1929 crisis, Monnet returned to Europe, where he continued to work as a businessman. He worked for months in Sweden as a liquidator for Kreuger & Toll after the financial empire of Ivar Kreuger had collapsed. Monnet had met Kreuger on several occasions in connection with the negotiations for the Polish and Romanian loans during the late 1920s. Yet Monnet refers to Kreuger as a 'disturbed man' whom he distrusted (Monnet 1978, 105). After his formidable swindle had been exposed to the whole world, Kreuger committed suicide in Paris in March 1932. Six months later, Monnet was hired by John Foster Dulles to protect the American creditors' interests in the Swedish company. Monnet was praised for his work but he resigned of his own volition in July 1933.

He caught the travel bug again later the same year and his business ventures took him to Kuomintang, China, where he had been invited by its finance minister to assist in realizing the international investment goals of the Chiang Kai-shek government. In China, Monnet secured agreement from various banks to establish the Chinese Finance Development Corporation, to provide capitalization for private and public projects. Restoration and development of China's rail and communications infrastructure was a main achievement. Monnet's accomplishments in China were based on his conviction that it was futile to invest foreign capital in China without Chinese participation. Co-investment would spread the risk and, most importantly, provide the Chinese with incentives to develop their own economic growth infrastructure. Monnet also met Chiang Kai-shek, whose wife told Monnet, 'The General likes you. He says there is something Chinese in you' (Monnet 1978, 113). We will never know what she meant, but Chinese history seems to have been distinguished by patience and tenacity – if not always by compromise.

In February 1935, Monnet and George Murnane – who was then partner in the investment bank Lee, Higginson and Company of Boston, announced the formation of a partnership to be known as Monnet, Murnane & Co. Monnet and Murnane first met each other during the First World War, when both were involved in the war effort in which Murnane served as deputy commissioner for the American Red Cross for France. The company received financial assistance from John Foster Dulles, and the busi-

ness of Monnet, Murnane & Co. was to exploit opportunities in international financial markets. Although the
head offices were in New York and Paris, the company was
initially – and curiously – established and registered under
Canadian law, in Charlottetown, Prince Edward Island, on
20 July 1935.[40] Its capital stock was worth $110,000, divided
into one thousand preference shares of $100 each and two
thousand ordinary shares of the par value of $5 each. It is
not clear why the French Monnet and the American Murnane chose Prince Edward Island as their locale, but Monnet's close relationship to Canada may have played a role
in their decision. To add to the mystery, Monnet's name
and signature are missing from the early documents such
as the letters patent formally incorporating the company
under the Prince Edward Island Joint Stock Company Act,
dated 20 July 1935. But then, Monnet's life and the work
of the partnership with Murnane during 1936–7 is not well
documented, probably because it was only a fleeting and
unremarkable enterprise among several. Thus, as Monnet
states in his memoirs, 'George Murnane and I worked on a
number of different projects of which I have only dim recollections' (Monnet 1978, 115).

However, on 31 August 1937 a decision was taken by the
directors to replace Monnet, Murnane & Co., Prince Edward
Island, with Monnet, Murnane & Co., Hong Kong (Hackett
2008). Lower taxation and looser regulations in Hong Kong
may have been the main reasons behind the move. Monnet,
Murnane & Co., Prince Edward Island, ceased to exist as
of 7 September 1937. Its termination was communicated to
the provincial secretary of Prince Edward Island in a letter
dated 12 April 1938.[41] This letter was signed by the company's president, Jean Monnet.

Threats of War

Although Monnet's partnership with Murnane was not formally dissolved until 1944, he had already become fully pre-

occupied by pressing world events towards the end of the
1930s. In the company of his friends, partners, and profes-
sional colleagues in international finance, namely George
Murnane and John Foster Dulles, Jean Monnet first assessed
the Nazi regime in September 1935 at a dinner party in
Long Island, New York. Dulles reported that Hitler's first
decrees against the Jews had just been published. Monnet
responded, 'A man who is capable of that will start a war'
(Monnet 1978, 116). More importantly, Monnet, like his
colleagues and opposite numbers from business in Canada,
responded by devoting his own organizational skills and talents, acquired from the private sector, to marshalling public
resources to combat and defeat the man who Monnet with
his usual prescience identified as capable of starting a war.

Monnet's success in combining his wartime and League
of Nations experience with private banking had attracted
much attention and admiration. However, Monnet was
ready to bid farewell to international finance: 'In fact, I was
growing bored with international finance, which ten years
earlier had seemed so vast and rewarding. By now, I found
the routine monotonous and the horizons narrow. The
whole of my attention was directed at the dangers that were
piling up in Europe and threatening world peace' (Monnet
1978, 115).

On 30 September 1938, British prime minister Neville
Chamberlain, French prime minister Édouard Daladier,
and Italian prime minister Benito Mussolini, met with German chancellor Adolf Hitler in Munich to discuss a 'just
solution' to the German-Czech Sudetenland controversy.
While Chamberlain seemed convinced that the Munich
Agreement would prevent military action and prevent a
war, Daladier was considerably more sceptical of Hitler's
intentions.

Monnet had first met Daladier in early 1938, when he was
minister of defence and, given Monnet's usual penchant
for making friends, they had become 'friendly' (Monnet
1978). Only four days after the Munich Agreement, Daladi-

er chaired a meeting that concluded that four thousand American warplanes were needed to improve the obsolete French air force. Monnet participated in the meeting, but Daladier had already decided that Monnet would be sent to Washington to convince the American president, Franklin Delano Roosevelt, to supply France's need for warplanes. Predictably, Monnet's knowledge of and experiences in the New World convinced Daladier that he had found the right man for the challenge to convince American isolationists of France's justifiable need.

Franklin Delano Roosevelt, Jean Monnet, and the Canadian Scheme

Isolationism was still prevalent and American production capacity was limited and insufficient to meet France's requests. However, Monnet shared Daladier's views. They were convinced that without an adequate air force, France would be a vulnerable target for Hitler's Wehrmacht and especially for the Luftwaffe. But then on 19 October 1938, Monnet was invited to meet with President Roosevelt at his private residence in Hyde Park, New York. The meeting was informal and confidential, apparently sponsored by William Bullitt, the US ambassador to France. Bullitt and Prime Minister Daladier knew each other very well, and it was Bullitt who advised Daladier to deploy Monnet for the task, given Monnet's familiarity and profound comprehension of America and North American ways, most of which, we can deduce from time spent, was derived from his Canadian experiences. And what an introduction! Bullitt presented Monnet as 'an intimate friend of mine for many years, whom I trust as a brother' (Duchêne 1994, 65). In a 1971 interview, Monnet explains that Bullitt and his father, Jean-Gabriel Monnet, had been close friends for many years.[42]

The meeting between President Roosevelt and Monnet was a meeting between two friends of Canada. Like Monnet, Roosevelt had enjoyed a special relationship with

Canada. Roosevelt had been a frequent visitor to Canada from the age of one. His parents vacationed with their children during summer months at Campobello Island in New Brunswick, Canada, but the island and their resort was accessible only through the state of Maine. To this day, residents of the island are often better off, logistically, shopping for even basic foodstuffs in the United States than on the island. Put otherwise, the island's lifeline is primarily through the United States, and there cannot be more intimate ties between Canada and the United States than those based on sustenance.

Later in life, Roosevelt acquired his own thirty-four-room 'cottage' on the island, where he vacationed and spent lengthy retreats both before and during his long tenure as president.[43] In fact, Campobello Island was the place where his son, Franklin Delano Roosevelt Jr, was born in 1914, and it was also there President Roosevelt fell ill with polio in 1921 while on vacation. Although the summer of 1939 was his last summer on the island, Roosevelt often acknowledged his intimate ties with Canada: 'I ... thank the people of Canada for their hospitality to all of us. Your course and mine have run so closely and affectionately during these many long years that this meeting adds another link to that chain. I have always felt at home in Canada.'[44]

It was during their meeting on 19 October 1938 that President Roosevelt and Monnet discussed what has been referred to as the 'Canadian Scheme,' a way around isolationism and understood as the possibility that France could buy American aircraft parts, which then could be assembled by a French company in Canada before being transported to France. The origin of the scheme is not entirely clear, but William Bullitt and Jean Monnet may have conceived of the idea together. Discussions between the two of them during the spring of 1938 had resulted in a draft entitled 'Note on the Possible Establishment of an Aeronautical Abroad out of Reach of Enemy Attack' (Monnet 1978, 117). What is clear, however, is that the initiative was appealing to both Monnet and Roosevelt. The president considered a cross-border location to be a convenient strategy because it was compatible with the American Neutrality Act of 1935, which forbade sales of weapons to belligerents. However, the initiative was also appealing to him because of his special relationship with Canada – one that Monnet shared as well. In Monnet's case, however, Canada was a source of creativity and inspiration to him in times of crisis.

President Roosevelt was so enthusiastic about the idea that he sketched a map of the US-Canada border identifying a possible location for the plant. At the end of the meeting, Monnet asked for the sketch as a souvenir and reminisced that 'without a moment's hesitation, without even bothering about what I might do with it, he handed it to me' (Monnet 1978, 119). Unfortunately, the prized memento of the remarkable get-together was lost during the Second World War when Monnet's papers were burnt during the German occupation. Forty years later, Monnet fondly remembered the 'exceptional confidence [Roosevelt] placed in a visitor he had just met for the first time' (1978, 119).

Indeed, Jean Monnet was very impressed with his first meeting with President Roosevelt. Monnet writes in his memoirs,

Roosevelt saw the United States in its world situation, and in his view the dangers that were massing in Europe were a threat to democracy in the New World as well as in the Old. That is why he welcomed a Frenchman of whom he knew little save the one thing that mattered to him: this foreigner had ideas about how we could combine to resist a common enemy. (Monnet 1978, 118)

Of course, Roosevelt foresaw Hitler as an alarming threat to the free world more than three years before he requested Congress to recognize a state of war between Germany and the United States in December 1941.

After the meeting with Roosevelt, Monnet and Bullitt met with the US secretary of the treasury, Henry Morgenthau

Jr, on 22 October to discuss the details. Morgenthau was sceptical towards the plan to establish an aircraft plant in Canada (Blum 1965). Morgenthau's relations with Monnet were complex, according to Hackett's analysis of Monnet's involvement with the Roosevelt administration (Hackett 2008). On the one hand, Morgenthau respected Monnet's experience, contacts, and astute judgment. On the other hand, Morgenthau suspected that Monnet had a darker side, given the gossip on Monnet he took pains to gather from his American business associates. Morgenthau, a dyed-in-the-wool Democrat, was an intensely political person who was suspicious about Monnet's close friendships with many Republicans. Additionally, Morgenthau regarded the New York financial community, of which Monnet was a member, as hostile to the New Deal (Hackett 1995a).

Notwithstanding Morgenthau's reservations, Monnet was able to pursue his plan for aircraft destined to France to be assembled in Canada and, in November 1938, a twenty page memorandum was presented to the French government.[45] The memorandum confirmed that two thousand planes would be delivered to France during 1939 if the orders were placed by the end of 1938.

The Memorandum

'Facilities to Be Established in Canada,' a subtitle of the memorandum written by Jean Monnet on 14 November 1938, states,

The plants to establish in Canada would essentially represent an insurance against an eventual interruption of delivery of airplanes ordered in the States, and in case of an application of the Neutrality Act. Therefore the Canadian plants should be conceived with a view to finish and assemble spare parts provided by American firms in a form as elaborated as will be permitted by such export restrictions as may be applied under the Neutrality Act. They may serve also eventually as a basis easily extensible in case of war.[46]

The memorandum also provides details on the production objectives of the Canadian plants:

So as to meet these requirements and at the same time limit the initial capital outlay to a minimum, the plants would be organised so as to have production yearly capacity on a 3 shift basis of say 2.500 planes but provisionally they would be run only on the basis of a current production of say 6 planes a week, this slow rhythm of production would be maintained from the date when the Canadian plants would be able to function until the time when deliveries of planes ordered in the States would be interrupted as a result of the Neutrality Act being applied. In that case the orders placed in U.S.A. would be completed in parts insofar as such parts would be allowed to be exported from the U.S. under the Neutrality Act, the Canadian plants taking then charge of the assembling and raising their production to the limit of their capacity. If the orders from U.S. were delivered without interference the production plants in Canada would be maintained on the basis of minimum output of 300 planes a year, thus keeping them as a basis to be used and developed in case of war for the prompt finishing and assembling of parts obtained from U.S. industry.[47]

The memorandum presented plans for organizing the Canadian plants along with costs:

It is proposed that the Canadian facilities be divided into two units for fabrication of air planes structures and one or two for the manufacture of motors and one or two for manufacture of propellers; if a Douglas bomber and a Curtiss pursuit plane were selected for manufacturing in U.S. and plants in Canada based originally for the assembling of these planes, then one motor factory only would be required because the Wright motor is used for both planes. The question of whether one or two propeller plants would be required would depend upon the number of types of propeller used. It is estimated that the initial capital outlay required for the establishment of these plants in Canada would be roughly between 20 and 25 million Dollars.[48]

And the location – most importantly the location – was not to be forgotten:

It is necessary to occupy the maximum of locations to which U.S. Labour can be attracted and where housing will be least difficult. In this connection it is to be noted that Canada is not generally highly developed industrially, it does not have any considerable supply of transient industrial labour, and its areas of considerable population are few. Also, locations must be selected where transportation to and from the U.S. side, without dependence upon lake transit, is essential. Thus, the desirable areas are seemingly limited to the Canadian areas opposite Buffalo New York, and Detroit Michigan. The Sault Sainte-Marie area lacks sufficient population, and the climate is over rigorous in winter. It is possible that some of the larger Canadian cities to the eastward of Detroit and Buffalo but not contiguous to the U.S. especially around Montreal may suffice for the location of activities such as propeller manufacture that do not require so numerous personnel.[49]

On 9 December, Prime Minister Daladier asked Monnet to go back to Washington to turn his proposals into planes (Duchêne 1994, 68). Monnet responded without hesitation and left the following day. In connection with this trip, Monnet also seized the opportunity to travel to Canada in order to advance the aircraft plant project (Hackett 2008, 116). However, in a meeting on the last day of 1938, Morgenthau told Monnet that the United States Army would be opposed to the Canadian scheme because the production of the planes would divulge classified American military information and that the Neutrality Act would be violated. The ever-distrustful Morgenthau also criticized the Canadian scheme to members of his own staff by posing the following question: 'How long do we know that Canada and England are going to be our allies?' (Haight 1970, 29).

The Canadian scheme was also met with scepticism by the American aviator and hero Charles Lindbergh, who at that time was spending time 'globe trotting among the capitals of Europe on government missions' (Berg 1999, 375). As a private individual in voluntary public service, Lindbergh had attended several meetings on the Canadian scheme, by invitation from his friend Ambassador Bullitt.[50] However, Lindbergh was an outspoken opponent of getting the US involved in European affairs: 'From the time the Canadian Plan was first outlined to me, I had reservations about the effect it would have on both America and Europe' (376). Lindbergh had been greatly impressed by the superiority of the German Luftwaffe, and to the astonishment of his colleagues at one of the meetings, Lindbergh instead suggested that France should purchase bombers, not from Canada, but from Germany! According to Berg, Lindberg argued that Hitler might actually 'welcome the opportunity to make a gesture to protect his western frontier' (376).

After Germany invaded Poland, Great Britain and France then declared war on Germany in September 1939. Faced with war in Europe, Roosevelt appeared before Congress and asked that the Neutrality Act be amended to lift the embargo on sending military aid to European countries. This time, Roosevelt prevailed over the isolationists and on 4 November the amended Neutrality Act of 1939 was passed. The relaxed neutrality legislation allowed for a more extensive arms trade with belligerent nations – nations participating in war – on a cash and carry basis, in effect ending the arms embargo. Attention then shifted to direct purchases of American combat planes, and the innovative Canadian scheme evaporated.[51]

Monnet, equipped with his favourite organizational tool, the balance sheet or the *bilan*, estimated that American production capacities had to be doubled or tripled to meet Allied need for aircraft.[52] He also argued that the Allies had to cooperate and pool resources and policies. More specifically, he recommended a joint British-French purchasing agency, based on the First World War model. Once again, Monnet's patience and tenacity would serve him well. In November 1939, Monnet was appointed chair of the Anglo-

French Coordinating Committee in London in 1939. It was also agreed that the French and British Purchase Commissions in Washington should be merged. The newly established Anglo-French Purchasing Board in the United States was chaired by Arthur B. Purvis, a Scot, who had moved to Canada where he had become president and managing director of Canadian Industries Ltd.[53]

One of Monnet's major achievements as chair of the Anglo-French Coordinating Committee was to persuade the British to join the French in submitting large joint orders for American aircraft in March 1940 (Duchêne 1994). But then after the collapse of France in the face of the Nazi onslaught in June 1940, Monnet was asked by Winston Churchill to move to Washington to continue the vital supply work for Britain as a member of the British Supply Council. Monnet complied. The British Supply Council consisted solely of representatives from British and Canadian ministries, including C.D. Howe, the Canadian minister of munitions and supply, plus Jean Monnet as the only 'member-at-large' (Rohmer 1978, 109). Even in company with C.D. Howe, once referred to as 'the greatest organizer Canada has ever seen' (see Bothwell and Kilbourn 1979, 148), Monnet excelled with his innovative contributions in stimulating American war production, which he was convinced was the most critical requirement for winning the war.

The levels of American war production actually achieved in 1942 and 1943 proved to be close to the goals that Monnet had deemed necessary in the fall of 1941 for victory. Robert R. Nathan, the American economist and an adroit chronicler of Monnet's contributions to the success of the Allies, asserts without qualification that without the efforts of Jean Monnet, the victory would most certainly 'have been delayed many months, with many more casualties' (1991, 67). Nathan's assertion most certainly substantiates Roosevelt's famous catchphrase, originally coined by Monnet: 'We must be the great arsenal of democracy.' The British economist John Maynard Keynes once remarked that Monnet, through his efforts and success in increasing American armament production, probably shortened the war by one year (Duchêne 1994). It was Monnet's remarkable capacity to influence important decision-makers that led to his highly successful contribution to America's mobilization.

As a Frenchman working for the British government in Washington, Jean Monnet had once again seen firsthand the results of what can be achieved if scarce resources are organized towards a common goal. And he also witnessed the devastating and absolutely horrific objectives that efficient, albeit evil, organization could achieve. It is no wonder that Monnet was in awe of organization. Fortunately, he was consumed by the potentially positive effects of organization and not its potentially nefarious results. Others in eminent positions recognized as much and so, while working for the Victory Program in Washington, Monnet was dispatched to Algiers in 1943 to join the French National Liberation Committee at the behest of President Roosevelt. And there with his recently acquired reverence for organization, mixed with his *theoria* of acquired virtue – patience, tenacity, and compromise – his vision of a federation or of a European entity among the states of Europe emerged.

Conclusion

Jean Monnet's contribution to the success of the Allied effort is immeasurable, as Hackett seems to suggest by identifying the importance of the progressively challenging tasks that Monnet assumed: 'From 1938 to 1945, Monnet went from being a buyer of aircraft for France, to chairman of the London-based Anglo-French Coordinating Committee, then a Washington member of the British Supply Council before going to Algiers as an informal representative for the Roosevelt administration' (Hackett 1995a, 25–6).

Although their encounters can be counted by the fingers on one hand, the relationship between Monnet and

President Roosevelt, two friends of Canada, forms what Scandinavians refer to as a *rød tråd* or a 'red thread' – a common thread – throughout this period, perhaps because their personalities were so much alike. After the president's death Eleanor wrote, 'Franklin's illness was another turning point, and proved to be a blessing in disguise; for it gave him the strength and courage he had not had before. He had to think out the fundamentals of living and learn the greatest of all lessons – infinite patience and never-ending persistence' (Nowlan 1975, 113). Eleanor could have been describing Jean Monnet.

At any rate, Monnet admired Roosevelt, who in his eyes personified the grandeur of public office, and when Roosevelt died in April 1945, Monnet actually wept (Fontaine 1991a).[54] Monnet was particularly impressed with the role President Roosevelt played in shifting America from isolationism to absolute involvement in winning the Second World War, for which the United States was to be the principal supplier and financier, an important source of military manpower, and, in the end, a leader in waging the war and planning the peace. This, Hackett remarks, 'was enough to dazzle even an experienced America-watcher like Monnet who had first been to the New World soon after the turn of the century and who lived and worked there on and off throughout his life' (1995a, 25). His first trip to the New World was to Canada in July 1907, but Monnet turned to Canada again when France and Europe had been challenged by the crisis of a world war.

5

Canada as Monnet's Early Inspiration and Lifelong Liaison

In this new world always on the move, I learned to get rid of the old atavistic suspicions which are so much a pointless worry and a waste of time ... Here, I encountered a new way of looking at things: individual initiative could be accepted as a contribution to general good.

Jean Monnet (1978, 46)

The final scenes in a film are not like those in a life's drama. The former can be preserved but the latter tend to fade into obscurity. Time does seem to have such an effect on life. But then as Reverend Jesse Jackson puts it with his usual pithy eloquence, 'Time is neutral and does not change things. With courage and initiative leaders change things' (Barker 1988, 212). Monnet changed things with courage and initiative. He was instrumental in creating what has now evolved into the European Union and, in turn, bringing prosperity and peace for Europeans.[55]

It takes courage to abandon 'old atavistic suspicions' because, although they may be 'a pointless worry and waste of time' to some, they are exceedingly comforting and empowering to many others – a phenomenon of which Monnet must have been well aware as he witnessed the scourge of his century: atavistic nationalism in Europe and elsewhere. He was certainly aware of the weaknesses – and the strengths – of the Old World and of the New World, which he referred to frequently in his memoirs. Indeed, Monnet's hallmark that distinguishes him from other great leaders and statesmen of the century is his characteristic meshing of the Old and New Worlds.

Monnet's Two Worlds

To Jean Monnet, the New World represented more than just a commercial opportunity and a lifeline in times of crisis. The New World was understood to complement the Old World in terms of his *theoria*, which involved a structured method of comparison to define, explain, and draw lessons from the similarities and differences of the two. Monnet was always open to new learning experiences. Thus, his purpose in comparing and contrasting the two Worlds was not to pass judgment on their respective values and ethics but to determine how the successful values, endemic to the practices in each, could complement and reinforce the other concretely. The values of the two were expressed in his vision for European unity.

Moreover, Monnet firmly believed that Europe and North America could and should be partners in a common project: world peace. In fact, in a short 1961 article Monnet argues for the creation of a far-reaching 'Atlantic community' in which the European nations, together with Canada and the United States, would share common institutions based on a genuine delegation of powers (Monnet 1961). 'Western Unity: The Cornerstone of World Peace' was written when Monnet was president of the Action Committee for the United States of Europe. It illustrates that Monnet did not consider a wider Atlantic community to be in conflict with his efforts on behalf of European unity. Rather, he saw European unity as a precondition for a 'true' Atlantic community, a fusion of the Old World and the New World where Europe and North America could act as equal partners. The article also displays the boundless confidence he had in governments – and the people they serve – to recognize a good deal. He was even 'convinced that ultimately, the United States too will delegate powers of effective action to common institutions, even on political questions' (Monnet 1961, 48), despite its deeply entrenched and almost sacred tradition of upholding states' rights. Perhaps this is why Duchêne (1991) argues that there are two main themes in Monnet's philosophy – or *theoria* to use this book's lexicon: first, European unity; and second, through Europe, the search for improved international government.

Jean Monnet's use of the concepts of Old World and New World, therefore, stands in sharp contrast to populist depictions of Europe and North America as distrustful of and even estranged from each other. Philippe Roger, a scholarly expert on anti-Americanism, notes that although France is the only major Western European nation-state that has never fought a war with the United States, it is the most 'strident' of the European states in its anti-American sentiment (2005). Even after 9/11, there was an upsurge in anti-Americanism in France (as well as in the rest of Europe), but particularly among the French intelligentsia. As if to deliberately make matters worse, the US secretary of defence, Donald Rumsfeld, disparaged all European opposition – and particularly French opposition – to his war plans as the opinion of 'Old Europe,' while indignant US senators and representatives demanded that government food service providers and restaurants in their states change the names of popular foods, like 'French fries' and 'French toast,' to 'freedom fries' and 'freedom toast' and so on. It is not that these widespread phobias were before Monnet's time. His generation endured more than its share of national phobias. Monnet was simply above it all.

Monnet loved both worlds and he saw no contradictions between the pooling of sovereignty in common institutions and his loyalty to and admiration of France. Monnet was passionately devoted to his country. In fact, his daughter, born in 1941, was named Marianne in homage to France's national symbol of reason, liberty, and the ideals of the republic. Monnet thought that the greatness of France would be consolidated through a united Europe and a strong Atlantic partnership. In 1961, *Time* magazine effectively encapsulated his perspective in this regard with its portrayal of him as 'the most dedicated internationalist of them all – although at the same time he remains as thoroughly French as Cognac, the town of his birth' (1961). The subtitle of an August 1944 *Fortune* magazine article captures the same duality: 'M. Jean Monnet of Cognac: Businessman, Banker, Expediter Extraordinary in Two Wars, He Stands for a France that Will Work in the Tradition of American Friendship' (Davenport 1944). Later and as a contemplative octogenarian, Monnet reflected on how he had relished *Fortune*'s complimentary depiction of him (Monnet 1978).

Over time, the French have realized that there is no contradiction between France and Europe, and that Foreign Minister Bidault's assertion in 1953 that France could *faire l'Europe sans défaire la France* (build Europe without undoing France) is valid (Drake 2008). The 1988 decision of the French government to place Monnet's remains to the Pantheon in Paris on the centennial of his birth – the highest honour that can be accorded the memory of a French citizen – demonstrates that he is esteemed by his compatriots as both a great Frenchmen and a great European. Actually, European integration is now a consensus issue in French politics and even the Gaullists seem to agree on the need for a united Europe in partnership with North America. Nicolas Sarkozy's 2009 decision to fully reintegrate France into all structures of the North Atlantic Treaty Organization are indicative of this trend.

Monnet's affection and admiration for North America is also evident. He lived in North America sporadically, but most often he was living there at crucial turning points in his life. Hackett claims that Jean Monnet, at least until after the Second World War, had more extensive knowledge of Canada and the United States and more friends in North America than he did in either France or elsewhere in Europe (Hackett 1995b). His North American friends became close and very dear friends to whom Monnet could appeal for support, financial or otherwise, at difficult times throughout his career. And they were always ready and willing to help out. Henry Kissinger once said that Monnet 'mesmerized' America's leading statesmen into seeing the world 'from his own unique perspective' (1982, 138). Charm indeed: somehow or other Monnet was a master of introducing 'European interests into American mechanisms' (Roussel 1996, 131).

However, Monnet apparently realized that charm was fleeting and that the key to lasting political change in Europe was through organization and through changing organizations, namely the nation-state. That took courage. He understood that nation-states and ultra-nationalism – ultra-atavism, if you will – had been the main source of conflict and concomitant suffering throughout Europe and beyond. Monnet believed that the deeply entrenched habits related to national sovereignty could be 'modified in the pressure chambers of new institutions,' as the French economist Robert Marjolin aptly put it (1991, 172). Supranational institutions were the remedy for the European disease: perennial conflict. In his 1952 speech to the Common Assembly, Monnet made it clear that institutions had to change:

The union of Europe cannot be based on goodwill alone. Rules are needed. The tragic events we have lived through and are still witnessing may have made us wiser. But men pass away; others will take our place. We cannot bequeath them our personal experience. That will die with us. But we can leave them institutions. The life of institutions is longer than that of men: if they are well built, they can accumulate the wisdom of succeeding generations. (Monnet 1978, 384)

But we have strayed from the Reverend Jackson's first characterization of leadership – courage – and neglected his second – initiative – which was a characteristic that Monnet also held in spades. When the time had come to act on an idea after long periods of patient waiting and deliberation, the course was simple for Jean Monnet: he just contacted the person who could give him what he wanted in order to realize his idea. It did not matter to Monnet whether it was the president of the United States or a bar manager in rural Canada. The advancement of his cause was his sole preoccupation, and, according Duchêne, Monnet had a 'sharp nose for real information and influence, irrespective of where they were located, high or low' (1991, 189–90) and an 'uncanny ability to by-pass the obstructions which prevent most people from passing through the bureaucratic labyrinth' (194).

It was not haughtiness or insensitivity to other people's busy schedules that made this direct approach so natural for him. Rather, it was a conviction that people would listen with interest if one had something important to say. Monnet never sat down for a discussion without a comprehensible message and an unambiguous proposal. To quote Monnet, 'Statesmen are concerned to do good, and above all to extricate themselves from awkward corners; but they do not always have either the taste or time for using their imagination. They are open to creative ideas, and anyone who knows how to present such ideas has a good chance of having them accepted' (Monnet 1978, 286–7). In times of crisis, he realized that truer words were never said. He viewed crises as singular opportunities for initiative and used them as constitutional moments, defined as 'the rare moments in the nation's history when deep, principled discussion transcends the logrolling and horse-trading of everyday majority politics' (Elster 1988, 6). These moments are produced generally by revolutions, social unrest, financial bankruptcy, or some other serious performance crisis, or follow from external shocks such as war, conquest, and defeat (Olsen 1997). As an individual with a clear idea, Monnet seized the many constitutional moments that his long life offered him. His initiative was relentless: 'Although it takes a long time to reach the men at the top, it takes little to explain to them how to escape from the difficulties of the present. This is something they are glad to hear when the critical moment comes. Then, when ideas are lacking, they accept yours with gratitude' (Monnet 1978, 231).

Initiative was certainly a requisite for travelling alone across Canada as teenager. However, both the pioneer atmosphere and his impressive achievements in the New World boosted his self-confidence and turned him into an assured and assertive young man. In Canada, Monnet was initiated to the self-possessed optimism that is peculiar to North America – a trait that is inclined to embrace change. Monnet sustained that trait throughout his entire career and beyond. His encounters with newly arrived immigrants from the Old World in the New World impressed Monnet and inspired him to consider possibilities for fundamental political change – an occurrence that has been noted previously: 'If we attempt to explain the success of Monnet's career we will discover that these early travels played an important role' (Bromberger and Bromberger 1969, 13).

Monnet's belief in individual initiative cannot easily be attached to a particular political ideology. Was his individualism, with its usual association to laissez-faire, related to a certain liberal perspective? Probably not. Throughout his life, he was an unwavering proponent of free trade – a principle normally connected to the concept of the limited state. However, Monnet was also a believer in central planning. In fact, he was France's post-war planner par excellence between 1945 and 1952 when he was responsible for the French Planning Commissariat, which reported directly to the prime minister. Ideologically, he seemed to have been his own man, and his independence from the constraints of a priori precepts seems to have been infectious. He managed to unite people normally associated with divergent political ideologies into a common cause. Fontaine praises Monnet in this regard because he apparently 'managed alone to span the gap between an Italian socialist and a British conservative, a Dutch antirevolutionary and a German social democrat – and all these politicians on one side, from all the labor unionists on the other' (1991a, 58).

Jean Monnet always seemed to mix individual initiative with teamwork, and he had a special talent when it came to mobilizing powerful groups and coalitions to support his ideas. He never worked alone, and Canada has been mentioned as a source of his collaborative style, a style that was blind to nationality and cultural distinction (Hermann 1968; Roussel 1996). Monnet also attached little importance to social status in dealing with people in both his private and public life. Berndt von Staden, the former *chef de Cabinet* to Walter Hallstein (president of the Commission to the European Communities from 1958 to 1967), once remarked,

Monnet was able to make a distinction between people of influence, and people who were well-informed. If it came to information, he did not hesitate a moment to call a very junior man and to ask him questions. Then he was quite willing to spend hours of his time, and his time was precious, with somebody who had no political influence of his own, but who was able to give him full background information and valuable advice. (Qtd in Duchêne 1991, 195–6).

As illustrated in chapter 2, it was a horse-lending blacksmith in Alberta in 1907 who gave Monnet his 'first lesson in pooling resources' (*Time* 1961).

Courage and initiative are featured in this chapter. Patience, compromise, and tenacity have been highlighted in previous chapters. David Johnson (2006), an astute analyst of Canadian public administration, points out what is obvious to anyone who has frequented an airport bookstore: there is a plethora of books on leadership cranked out by apparently successful private sector executives. Johnson distils their recipes for successful leadership into four distinctive attributes, which can be presented in their shorthand version: first, vision, mission, and accountability; second, flexibility; third, the promotion of teamwork; and finally, 'the ability to anticipate, respond to, and take advantage of change' (Johnson 2006, 641). As this book has demonstrated, Monnet fully possessed all of these four qualities, but what distinguishes him from business leaders and public sector leaders relates to the fourth element. He was certainly able to 'anticipate, respond to, and take advantage of change,' but even more significantly he possessed the ability to initiate change, and not just ordinary change, but paradigmatic change.

When Canadian and European policy analysts assess the causes of paradigmatic change, the general conclusion seems to be that policies do not change by an abrupt shift but rather through slow organic processes of 'historical drift' (Hall 1993; Olsen 2007; Skogstad 2008). It is easy to agree with such an observation.[56] The creation of the European Coal and Steel Community in 1951 should be situated in a sequence of events in a slow-moving causal process stretching over extended periods in Jean Monnet's life. This perspective is also compatible with what Paul Pierson (2004) refers to as a 'motion picture' view rather than a 'snapshot' view of political life. And it is compatible with a perspective that identifies leadership, transformed into statesmanship, as the catalyst for slow-moving processes that culminate in paradigmatic change.

But this perspective is incomplete. Micro- and even macro-changes may be affected by broad socio-economic forces, but it seems that, on the basis of this study of Jean Monnet, comprehensive change, the slow-moving paradigmatic change, an accumulation of individual achievements, can be brought on by just that: individual achievement. The accomplishments of great leaders have been left to historians to discover while political scientists and policy analysts tend to focus on broad and usually ineluctable factors and trends as influencing governance. Such factors do influence political orders but so do outstanding individuals, like Jean

Monnet. Above all, Monnet was a master of political design, and the successful establishment of the European Coal and Steel Community was due in large part to his extraordinary ability to identify and exploit opportunities for institutional design (Ugland 2009). There are, therefore, important lessons to be drawn from Jean Monnet for European leaders and prospective designers at the EU level.

Monnet's Canadian Legacy

Monnet always seemed more concerned with practical achievements than with his reputation and honours and awards. His lifelong friend Dwight Morrow, who worked with Monnet in London during the First World War, once said that 'there are two kinds of people – those who want to be someone, and those who want to do something' (Monnet 1978, 519). According to Morrow, Monnet clearly belonged to the latter kind. For instance, it never seemed to bother Monnet that his Coal and Steel proposal – which practically bore his imprint in indelible ink – will forever be known as the Schuman Plan. In May 1950, Monnet was responsible for and fully preoccupied with the French Reconstruction Plan. So the most important issue for him was that the first step towards supranational European unity had been taken and not that his colleague's surname had been stamped on the plan, seeming to bestow Schuman with sole credit for this stroke of genius. Furthermore, Monnet was never preoccupied with official titles, pomp, or ceremony. He felt that such trappings involved limitations on his freedom to act in favour of his own ideas. This is probably why he never ran for office. His exchange with an interviewer and writer for *Fortune* magazine in 1944 is revealing in this regard:

At the beginning of the summer, I was visited in Foxhall Road by a reporter from *Fortune* magazine, John Davenport. 'We want to tell your story,' he said. 'I've all the time in the world, so let's begin at the beginning.' For the first time, I turned back to look back on my past life, and was presented to the magazine's readers as 'M. Jean Monnet of Cognac.' I was fifty-six years old; and my career looked variegated and spasmodic. This disconcerted the authors of 'profiles' or *curricula vitae*, who were anxious to put me in some familiar category: politician, businessman, economist, diplomat, etc. I cared little for such definitions. (Monnet 1978, 221)

In an interview in 1970, Monnet even confirmed that he did not enjoy the title 'father of Europe.'[57] At the age of eighty-one, he said, tongue-in-cheek, that the moniker made him feel old! 'Son of Europe' would have pleased him more! In a subsequent interview a year later, Monnet was somewhat dismissive when asked about the European Communities' paternity: 'Il y a beaucoup de pères.'[58]

Despite Monnet's seeming disinterest in his legacy, both the EU and his name continue to enjoy a very special relationship with Canada. In fact, Canada is one of the EU's oldest and closest partners. Canadian–EU cooperation dates back to 1959 when the two political entities signed the Agreement for Cooperation in the Peaceful Uses of Atomic Energy. In October 2008, Canadian prime minister Stephen Harper and French president Nicolas Sarkozy, and then-president of the European Council, jointly announced talks on trade liberalization between Canada and the EU, talks that could lead to an 'ambitious' and 'truly historic' economic partnership.[59]

Jean Monnet's name and his Canadian legacy are particularly evident within academia, thanks to the Jean Monnet Action, a European Commission initiative that was launched in 1990 in his honour. Its purpose, according to the commission, is to stimulate 'teaching, research and reflection on European integration at higher education institutions throughout the world.'[60] It supports projects on five continents, and the program reaches up to 250,000 students every year. Between 1990 and 2008, Jean Monnet Action helped to set up 134 Jean Monnet European centres of excellence and 798 Jean Monnet university chairs worldwide. In 2006, the Delegation of the European Commission to Canada announced the creation of four EU centres of excellence at universities in Canada: University of Toronto, Carleton University, Université de Montréal / McGill University, collectively, and Dalhousie University. Besides these institutional grants, several Canadian universities have been awarded Jean Monnet chairs. In fact, the first Jean Monnet chair in European integration outside the EU was awarded to Professor Panayotis Soldatos at Université de Montréal in Canada in 1992. Thanks to Jean Monnet Projects funding, the academic field of European studies is flourishing in Canada, and as Amy Verdun – herself a Jean Monnet chair ad personam – so succinctly expresses it, 'Jean Monnet support has brought Canadians closer to one another thereby facilitating knowledge about one another's research, teaching and outreach' (Verdun 2009).

Jean Monnet's legacy has been celebrated and honoured in France and by the European Union. However, it may not be so well known that individual nations, beneficiaries of Monnet's statecraft, have taken it upon themselves to honour him in the manner accorded customarily to national – and now rare supranational – luminaries: by way of the post office. During the Monnet centenary in 1988, many nations paid tribute to Jean Monnet by issuing commemorative stamps: Belgium, France, Germany, Luxembourg, Monaco, Portugal, and Spain. This was the second time Germany issued a stamp in honour of Jean Monnet. A German stamp was also issued in 1977 to mark the decision of the European heads of state and government to proclaim Jean Monnet the first 'honorary citizen of Europe' in 1976. This was the only stamp Jean Monnet saw before he died. In addition, France and Luxembourg issued stamps in 1980 after his death in 1979. In 2007, even the Republic of Guinea issued a new stamp as a mark of respect for Monnet on the occasion of the fiftieth anniversary of the Treaty of Rome.

The importance of stamps as honorific remuneration for

outstanding accomplishments is rarely lost on those with a keen sense of history, particularly on those who can appreciate historical agents of change. The importance of stamps certainly was not lost on Anne Morton, archivist at the Hudson's Bay Company Archives in Manitoba, who justifiably took umbrage at those nations – Britain in particular – not included in the 1988 list of national philatelic celebrants. In a 1989 open letter to the British magazine *Encounter*, she disparaged Britain's neglect of the Jean Monnet anniversary and particularly its philatelic neglect of Jean Monnet: 'It does seem a pity that Britain should not have so much as issued a postage stamp to commemorate the centenary of Jean Monnet's birth.' She did, however, encourage Britain to redress its oversight: 'Now that the 75th anniversary of the Great War is upon us perhaps readers might want to know something of what it was that Monnet did for the Allies in that war and the improbable means through which he did it.'[61]

Anne Morton then drew attention to Monnet's role in the First World War and indicated that interested parties could find more records and files about Monnet in the Hudson's Bay Company Archives in Winnipeg. With a reference to the cherished archives, she concluded, 'It seems right that they should be here, for it was in part Monnet's admiration for Winnipeg and Winnipeggers, "tough men in a tough climate," that started the whole extra-ordinary business in the first place.'[62]

To be sure, these new Canadians displayed the same Canadian courage and initiative as did Monnet in initiating a European union. If Monnet possessed those characteristics prior to his early Canadian adventure, they must have been reinforced during it. If he did not already possess characteristics in full measure, they certainly must have been imbued by virtue of his *theoria*, as Anne Morton suggests. The Advisory Committee that guides Canada Post in selecting stamp subjects should be so informed.

So much for images! What a script for a film! But Jean

Monnet, like genuinely great men and women, seemed to possess a certain modesty and was reluctant to sing his own praises. More often than not, he seemed inclined to understate his virtues. So it is little wonder that Monnet took so long to record his memoirs. His notes reveal that he had long been encouraged by many to put pen to paper and that he had made numerous attempts to write them (Rieben, Camperio-Tixier, and Nicod 2004). However, he never seemed ready. So not surprisingly, Monnet was well into his eighth decade before he managed to see the connections between and among the multitude of singularly important frames that, once strung together, constituted his life and its phenomenal effects. François Fontaine, who collaborated with Monnet in the writing of his life story, explains:

It was at this time – he was eighty-four – that he discovered the thread that had linked his intermittent activities, the thread that, if one went back in time, joined together Europe and the modernization of France, union among Frenchmen during the war, the Program for Victory, the Allied committees of 1940 and those of 1914. Then he realized he needed to go further back, as far as Cognac where his destiny was really earthed. Memories of the family table revived elements that were missing in a picture whose perspectives were still unclear in his mind. At bottom, he was not sure that he had led his life with any spirit and continuity. He justified his detours in his path by the sense of necessity which in his eyes, had been his chief driving force. 'I had no choice,' he often said by way of explanation. It was an insufficient one. When he had a better view of the overall picture and the chronology had been tied up, he saw that he had always looked for the same thing: to unite people. (Fontaine 1991a, 24)

It may have been at the family kitchen table that Monnet was asked to go to Canada in 1907. Pure chance, perhaps, but then some men do not believe in taking chances, even when they can learn something. Monnet was not one of them. He alone transformed his first long voyage to Canada into a learning experience, an inspirational model, and an enduring reference as he strived to unite diverse people in peace and prosperity, a struggle that still continues through the most remarkable international political integration project the world has ever known: the European Union.

Chronology
Jean Omer Marie Gabriel Monnet

1888 Born in Cognac, France.

1904 Travelled to London, England, to begin a two-year business apprenticeship.

1907 Went to Canada, where he travelled extensively between 1907 and 1914 to promote J.G. Monnet & Co. Cognac.

1914 Joined the liaison mission of the French Civil Supplies Service in London, England.

1919 Appointed deputy secretary-general of the League of Nations.

1922 Resigned from the League of Nations and returned to Cognac to save the family company, J.G. Monnet & Co. Cognac, from bankruptcy.

1926 Started a career as an international investment banker, which lasted until 1939. Worked on projects in Bulgaria, China, France, Poland, Romania, Sweden, and the United States.

1934 Married Silvia de Bondini in Moscow, Russia.

1935 Founded a business partnership with George Murnane – Monnet, Murnane & Co. – which was dissolved in 1944.

1939 Appointed president of the Franco-British Coordination Committee in London, England.

1940 Sent to the United States by the British government to join the British Supply Council in Washington, DC.

1943   Became a member of the National Liberation Committee of the Free French government in exile in
Algiers, Algeria.

1945   Appointed by the French Cabinet to head the
French Planning Commissariat.

1950   Monnet's Coal and Steel Community proposal was
presented to the French Cabinet in Paris by the
foreign minister, Robert Schuman, on 9 May. The
Schuman Plan was approved by the Cabinet and
later the same day announced to the press. Monnet was appointed chairman of the Schuman Plan
conference and head of the French delegation, in
a process that culminated with the signing of the
Treaty of Paris establishing the European Coal and
Steel Community on 18 April 1951.

1952   Appointed president of the High Authority of the
European Coal and Steel Community – a position
he held until 1955.

1955   Established the Action Committee for the United
States of Europe, where he served as head until it
was dissolved in 1975. Published his book *Les États-
Unis d'Europe ont commencé.*

1960   Sold his last holding in J.G. Monnet & Co. Cognac.

1976   Declared the first honorary citizen of Europe. Monnet's *Memoires* was published in French.

1978   The English translation of his memoirs was published.

1979   Died in his home – Houjarray – outside Paris. He
was buried in the village cemetery in Bazoches-sur-
Guyonne.

1988   On the centenary of his birth, Monnet's remains
were transferred to the Pantheon in Paris to
acknowledge the honour Monnet had given to
France.

Notes

1 Article 2, Association Statutes, Jean Monnet Association. The association was originally entitled Friends of Jean Monnet Association but was renamed in 1990.
2 Robert R. Bowie, interview, 15 June 1981, Washington, DC, Jean Monnet Foundation for Europe (JMFE), Lausanne.
3 Jean Monnet to Pierre Dupuy, 5 Dec. 1962, AMK 28/1/117, JMFE.
4 The Allan Line was founded in 1854 as the Montreal Ocean Steamship Company (Bonsor 1980). The company was later known as the Allan Line after one of its founders, Hugh Allan. The Allan Line name was used until the company was bought by the Canadian Pacific Railway in 1917. From that date, all Allan Line ships were integrated into the Canadian Pacific Line. The main transatlantic routes of the Allan Line were Liverpool, Quebec, and Montreal in the summer, and Liverpool to Saint John in the winter. The 10,757-ton *Virginian* was a very modern ship for its time when it entered service on 6 April 1905, and it was used in various capacities until 1955, when it was scrapped in Trieste, Italy.
5 As a historical aside, Mansfield was best known for his performances in Shakespeare plays and for his portrayal of the dual title roles in *Strange Case of Dr Jekyll and Mr Hyde*. And what a performer! While Mansfield was performing in 1888, Jack the Ripper was murdering prostitutes in London. According to Ripper expert Donald Rumbelow (1988), one

of Mansfield's fans wrote to the police accusing him of the murders. Apparently, the admirer could not believe that any actor could make so convincing a stage transformation from a gentleman into a mad killer without being homicidal. Mansfield was also a character and initial Ripper suspect in the 1988 TV movie *Jack the Ripper*.

In July 1907, Richard Mansfield returned from the United Kingdom with severe health problems (*New York Times* 1907), and he died shortly afterward on 30 August of liver cancer in New London, Connecticut, when he was only fifty years old.

6 This sale represents the beginning of a turbulent period in the company's history. In 1987, J.G. Monnet & Co. Cognac was sold to another German company – Asbach, Rüdesheim – before it was taken over by the Hennessy Group in 1991. Soon afterward (1992–3), Hennessy sold J.G. Monnet & Co. Cognac to one of its subsidiaries, Thomas Hine & Co., based in Jarnac, France. Today, J.G. Monnet & Co. Cognac is owned by Angostura Limited (CL Financial Limited), Trinidad and Tobago, after the company acquired Thomas Hine & Co. in 2003. Monnet Cognac is still produced, and, according to a representative from Thomas Hine & Co., the major markets of Monnet & Co. cognacs are in Asia, Russia, and the Scandinavian countries – and at a smaller level in New Brunswick, Canada.

7 Jean Monnet's parents, Maria Demelle Monnet (1868–1956) and Jean-Gabriel Monnet (1855–1939), had four children: Jean (1888–1979), Gaston (1890–1927), Henriette (1894–1991), and Marie Louise (1901–88). Together, the six have been said to form a traditional Charente family at the turn of the twentieth century, where 'the boys go into the cognac trade with the father; the girls stay with the mother to help in the solid homestead which often hosts the firm's customers for lunch, dinner and even overnight visits' (Hackett 2008, 5).

8 Passenger List 1865–1922, T491, RG76, Library and Archives Canada, Ottawa.

9 Parts of the bridge collapsed a second time in 1916, killing ten

more workers, before it was finally completed and opened for traffic in 1917.

10 The earliest reference to HBC dealing in UVPC brandy dates back to 5 January 1896. See Series of London Letterbooks – General, A. 5/66, fo. 65, Hudson's Bay Company Archives (HBCA), Winnipeg.

11 From their bases in Cape Breton, Nova Scotia, the Italian inventor Guglielmo Marconi sent the first wireless transmission across the Atlantic in 1902, and the Scottish Alexander Graham Bell launched the first manned flight in the British Empire in 1909.

12 It is worth mentioning that Monnet's hotel, the 450-room Royal Alexandra, completed the year before Monnet arrived, was the pride of the Canadian Pacific Railway. It closed in 1967 and was demolished in 1971. However, after being stored for more than twenty-five years, in 1999, the inventory from the old café, fittingly referred to as the European Dining Room, was purchased by the Canadian Museum of Rail Travel in Cranbrook, British Columbia. The museum recreated the entire room in 2004, including the vaulted ceiling, incorporating it into the museum facilities as the Royal Alexandra Hall.

13 Monnet once said that he based his judgment 'on the wisdom of practical men' (Monnet 1978, 271). Monnet identified the American economist and political scientist Walt W. Rostow as one of these men. Rostow also served as a central adviser on national security under both the John F. Kennedy and Lyndon B. Johnson administrations.

14 This quote is from Monnet's proposal as it was presented to the French government in April 1950. This proposal was presented by Schuman on 9 May 1950 with only minor modifications.

15 The adverse effects of alcohol consumption also came under increasing scrutiny in Monnet's homeland at the turn of the century. Absinthe, in particular, seemed to become a scapegoat for all evils in society and was prohibited in 1915. The consumption of wine was, however, considered to be accept-

able, and even French temperance leaders could themselves be winemakers (see, for instance, Brennan 1989; Prestwich 1979; Ugland 2003).

16 Series of London Letterbooks.

17 Robert Kindersley, governor of the HBC from 1915 to 1925, had many ties to Canada. He was a major shareholder in the Canadian National Railway, and the town of Kindersley, Saskatchewan, is named after him. Charles Sale succeeded Kindersley as the twenty-ninth governor of the HBC and stayed at this post until 1931.

18 Telegram, Jean Monnet to J.G. Monnet & Co., 25 Sept. 1910; telegram, Jean Monnet to J.G. Monnet & Co., 13 Oct. 1910, Hennessy Archive (HA), Cognac, France.

19 In connection with the 300th anniversary of the Hudson's Bay Company in 1970, the headquarters were moved from London to Winnipeg.

20 Agreement between the United Vineyard Proprietors Company of Cognac, J.G. Monnet & Co., and the Hudson's Bay Company, A 102/452, HBA.

21 Richard Burbidge is an important figure in the history of retailing as well as in the HBC. He is famous for developing Harrods in London into one of the most successful department stores in the world. Under his leadership, in 1898 Harrods introduced the first escalators to a delighted public. According to the HBC's website, newspapers of the day referred to shoppers being 'whisked away' to upper floors, as if by a 'magic carpet' (HBC 2009). Richard Burbidge was elected to the Board of the HBC in 1910, and his vision of the modern department store significantly influenced the development of the HBC's retail division. His son, Herbert Burbidge, became the first commissioner of stores in the reorganized HBC.

22 Jean Monnet to his father, Jean-Gabriel Monnet, 17 Feb. 1911, HA.

23 Agreement between the United Vineyard Proprietors Company of Cognac, J.G. Monnet & Co., and the Hudson's Bay Company.

24 Jean-Gabriel Monnet to N.H. Bacon, 12 Dec. 1911, A 102/
452, HBCA.

25 H.E. Burbidge, stores commissioner, Hudson's Bay Company, to Jean Monnet, 18 Sept. 1911, A 102/452, HBCA.

26 Census of Canada, 1921, table 26, 2:124.

27 Censuses of Canada, 1891–1971.

28 Although most famous for his evangelistic and temperance
work, John Marchant Whyte was one of the most productive
hymn writers in Canadian musical history, with several hundred songs to his credit. Together with his brother, David
Albert Whyte, he published three hymn collections: *Sing Out
the Glad News* (1885), *Songs of Calvary* (1889), and *Battle Songs
of the Cross* (1901) (Kallmann, Potvin, and Winters 1992).

29 Acute appendicitis is characterized by inflammation of the
appendix, and all cases require its removal. During the first
half of the twentieth century its incidence rose, particularly
in Europe, North America, and Australasia so that up to 16
per cent of the population had an appendectomy. In the last
three decades of the century, its incidence fell (Duggan and
Duggan 2006). The mortality rate associated with appendicitis also declined after the introduction of antibiotics and
the development of anaesthesia and improvements in care
before and after the operation.

30 Jean Monnet was always very close to his mother, perhaps
because they were few years apart in age. Maria Demelle
Monnet was only nineteen years old when Jean was born.
Talking about his parents, Monnet said in his memoirs, 'I
may have my father's imagination. But my mother taught
me that nothing can be achieved unless it is built on reality'
(Monnet 1978, 37).

31 Mr Chapon to Jean Monnet, 3 Apr. 1913, HA.

32 Georges Berthoin was chief representative of the Commission of the European Community to the United Kingdom from 1971 to 1973. In 2001, he was elected honorary
president of the Jean Monnet Association.

33 Minutes of the Meetings of Governor and Committee,
28 Mar. 1922, 211–14, A.1/265, HBCA.

34 Ibid.

35 Minutes of Meetings of Governor and Committee, 23 Sept. 1930, 159, A.1/170, HBCA.

36 In the 1958 classic *Organizations*, James G. March and Herbert A. Simon distinguish between two main lines of development in traditional organization theory (March and Simon 1993). The first, which derives from the work of Frederick W. Taylor, focuses upon the basic physical activities involved in production. The second is more concerned with the grand organizational problems of departmental division of work and coordination, a topic that became increasingly fashionable during the late 1930s and 1940s. Monnet would have been affected by both waves.

37 During the Second World War, Clarence Decatur 'C.D.' Howe, Canadian minister of munitions and supply, was responsible for organizing industrial resources to meet the needs of wartime. In these efforts, Howe recruited and relied heavily on talent ranked at the top of their professions and business enterprises. The so-called C.D. Howe Boys included prominent figures like Henry Borden, Robert Alexander Cecil 'R.A.C.' Henry, Gordon Scott, and Edward Plunket 'E.P.' Taylor (Bothwell and Kilbourn 1979, 131).

38 Jean Monnet admired Foster Dulles for his strength of character and his moral authority: 'I have always known him as decisive and inflexibly determined, just as history paints him, and at the same time warm, fond of good living, and an affectionate friend. One day the world will come to see him, alongside Eisenhower, as a man of great stature, a symbol of willpower that aroused conflicting passions. But this was not Foster Dulles the man. The Dulles I knew and loved was like many other men, but greater and more upright than most' (Monnet 1978, 105).

39 George W. Ball was undersecretary of state in the Kennedy and Johnson administrations. About Ball, Monnet once said, 'I profited greatly from his talents as a lawyer, blending the most concrete practicality with the very broadest concern for the general interest' (Monnet 1978, 227).

40 File 285, subseries 6, series 11, RG7, Archives of Prince
    Edward Island (APEI), Charlottetown, Prince Edward Island.
41 Jean Monnet, president of Monnet, Murnane, & Co., to prov-
    incial secretary of the Province of Prince Edward Island,
    12 Apr. 1938, APEI.
42 Interview with Jean Monnet by Alan Watson, 15 and 16 Nov.,
    2 and 3 Dec. 1971, AML 313/1 to 313/265, JMFE.
43 The cottage remained in the hands of the Roosevelts until
    1952. However, President Roosevelt's name is firmly attached
    to the island. For instance, the Franklin Delano Roosevelt
    Bridge connects Campobello Island to the eastern tip of
    the United States. This bridge was built in 1962, and Roos-
    evelt International Park was created on the island in 1964.
    Although it is a Canadian island, the park is maintained
    jointly by American and Canadian authorities.
44 Franklin D. Roosevelt address at Ottawa, 25 Aug. 1943, The
    American Presidency Project, http://www.presidency.ucsb
    .edu/ws/?pid=16448.
45 Memorandum from Jean Monnet, 14 Nov. 1938, AME 7/1/1,
    JMFE.
46 Ibid.
47 Ibid.
48 Ibid.
49 Ibid.
50 There was also a special link between Lindbergh and Mon-
    net, as the former was married to Anne Morrow, daughter
    of Monnet's close friend Dwight Morrow, former US senator
    and ambassador to Mexico. Monnet had worked with Mor-
    row in London during the First World War.
51 The neutrality policy came to its demise with the Lend-Lease
    Act of March 1941, which allowed the United States to sell,
    lend, or give war materials to allied nations.
52 The 'balance sheet' was an instrument Monnet used through-
    out his long career to organize his own thoughts, but also to
    convince others. During the Second World War, the balance
    sheet 'was an assessment – often in tabular form – of arma-
    ments, supplies, output and so forth' (Duchêne 1994, 74).

53 Arthur B. Purvis became a casualty of war when his plane crashed on take-off from Prestwick Airport in Scotland in August 1941. According to Jean Monnet, Purvis 'served the Allied war effort magnificently until his death' (Monnet 1978, 130).

54 Jean Monnet honoured the memory of Roosevelt by keeping a framed photo of the president in his bedroom at Houjarray for many years.

55 Jean Monnet has also been a source of inspiration for regional cooperation and trading blocs outside Europe. The African Union, for instance, although in its infancy, does have an institutional configuration similar to the one adopted by the European Coal and Steel Community.

56 This is certainly an observation that Monnet agreed with himself. In fact, Monnet often compared the path towards European political unity with the Norwegian adventurer Thor Heyerdahl's daring drift over the Pacific Ocean in his raft in 1947: 'It was the *Kon-Tiki*, whose adventure had thrilled the whole world, and which for me was a symbol of our own' (Monnet 1978, 524). Heyerdahl's book, *The Kon-Tiki Expedition* (1950), was published the same year as the Schuman Plan was presented. Today, visitors can see a copy of this book lying on the bedside table in Monnet's old home, Houjarray.

57 Interview with Jean Monnet by Georges Suffert, 10 and 11 May 1970, AML 298/1, JMFE.

58 Interview with Jean Monnet by Alan Watson.

59 News release, Harper hails agreement to work toward Canada-EU economic partnership, 17 Oct. 2008, Canadian Press.

60 From the official website of the European Commission, http://ec.europa.eu/education/lifelong-learning-programme/doc88_en.htm.

61 Anne Morton to *Encounter*, 10 July 1989, HBCA.

62 Ibid.

References

Almond, G.A. 1990. *A discipline divided: Schools and sects in political science*. Newbury Park, CA: Sage.

Ardagh, J. 1968. *The new French revolution: A social & economic survey of France 1945–1967*. London: Secker & Warburg.

Artibise, A.F.J. 1975. *Winnipeg: A social history of urban growth, 1874–1914*. Montreal: McGill-Queen's University Press.

Ball, G.W. 1978. Introduction. In *Memoirs*, ed. J. Monnet, 11–14. Garden City, NY: Doubleday.

– 1982. *The past has another pattern*. New York: Norton.

Barker, Lucius Jefferson. 1988. *Our time has come: A delegate's diary of Jesse Jackson's 1984 presidential campaign*. Urbana: University of Illinois Press.

Bellan, R. 1978. *Winnipeg, first century: An economic history*. Winnipeg: Queenston House.

Berg, A.S. 1999. *Lindbergh*. New York: Berkley Books.

Bill, C.P. 1901. Notes on the Greek qewros and qewria. *Transactions and Proceedings of the American Philological Association* 32: 196–204.

Blum, J.M. 1965. *From the Morgenthau diaries: Years of urgency 1938–1941*. Boston: Riverside / Houghton Mifflin.

Bonsor, N.R.P. 1980. *North Atlantic seaway*. Jersey: Brookside.

Bothwell, R., and W. Kilbourn. 1979. *C.D. Howe: A biography*. Toronto: McClelland and Stewart.

Brennan, T. 1989. Towards the cultural history of alcohol in France. *Journal of Social History* 23 (1): 71–92.

Brinkley, D., and C. Hackett, eds. *Jean Monnet: The path to European unity*. New York: St Martin's.

Bromberger, M., and S. Bromberger. 1969. *Jean Monnet and the United States of Europe*. New York: Coward-McCann.

Brook, T. 2008. *Vermeer's hat: The seventeenth century and the dawn of the global world*. Toronto: Viking Canada.

Burgess, M. 2009. Federalism. In *European integration theory*, ed. A. Wiener and T. Diez, 25–44. Oxford: Oxford University Press.

Burpee, L.J. 1948. Hudson's Bay Company. In *The encyclopedia of Canada*, ed. A. Shortt and A.G. Daughty, 3:212–15. Toronto: University Associates of Canada.

Coates, C.W., and Brothers. 1874. *The Canadian musical fountain for temperance meetings, bands of hope, temperance conventions, social gatherings, home circle, & c.* Toronto: Campbell.

Cook, R. 1986. *Canada, Quebec, and the uses of nationalism*. Toronto: McClelland and Stewart.

Creighton, D. 1970. *Canada's first century, 1867–1967*. Toronto: Macmillan Canada.

Davenport, J. 1944. M. Jean Monnet of Cognac. *Fortune* 30 (3): 120–5.

Dedman, M.J. 1996. *The origins and development of the European Union: A history of European integration*. London: Routledge.

Dinan, D. 1999. *Ever closer union*. 2nd ed. Boulder: Rienner.

Drake, H. 2008. The European Fifth Republic. *Contemporary French and Francophone Studies* 12 (2): 193–201.

Drucker, P.F. 1994. *Post-capitalist society*. New York: Harper Business.

– 1999. *Management challenges for the 21st century*. New York: Harper Collins.

Duchêne, F. 1991. Jean Monnet's methods. In Brinkley and Hackett, 184–209.

– 1994. *Jean Monnet: The first statesman of independence*. New York: Norton.

Duggan, J.M., and A.E. Duggan. 2006. Acute appendicitis. In *The epidemiology of alimentary diseases*, 91–4. Dortrecht: Springer.

Elster, J. 1988. Introduction. In *Constitutionalism and democracy*, ed. J. Elster and R. Slagstad, 1–18. Oslo: Scandinavian University Press.

Finer, S.E. 1997. *The history of government.* 3 vols. Oxford: Oxford University Press.

Fontaine, F. 1991a. Forward with Jean Monnet. In Brinkley and Hackett, 1–66.

– 1991b. Jean Monnet's methods. In Brinkley and Hackett, 184–209.

Fransen, F.J. 2001. *The supranational politics of Jean Monnet: Ideas and origins of the European community.* Westport: Greenwood.

Gagan, D.P., and R.R. Gagan. 2002. *For patients of moderate means: A social history of the voluntary public general hospital in Canada, 1890–1950.* Montreal: McGill-Queen's University Press.

Hackett, C.P. 1995a. Jean Monnet and the Roosevelt administration. In *Monnet and the Americans: The father of a united Europe and his U.S. supporters,* ed. C. Hackett, 25–69. Washington, DC: Jean Monnet Council.

– 1995b. *Monnet and the Americans.* Washington, DC: Jean Monnet Council.

– 2008. *A Jean Monnet chronology: Origins of the European Union in the life of a founder, 1888 to 1950.* Washington, DC: Jean Monnet Council.

Haight, John McVickar Jr. 1970. *American aid to France, 1938–1940.* New York: Atheneum.

Hall, P.A. 1993. Policy paradigms, social learning, and the state: The case of economic policymaking in Britain. *Comparative Politics* 25 (3): 275–96.

HBC. 2009. Our history: People. Builders: Richard Burbidge. http://www.hbc.com/hbcheritage/history/people/builders/burbidge.asp.

Hermann, L. 1968. *Jean Monnet: Un portrait.* Paris: Editions Dalloz.

Heyerdahl, Thor. 1950. *The Kon-Tiki expedition: By raft across the South Seas.* London: Allen & Unwin.

Holland, M. 1996. Jean Monnet and the federal functionalist approach to the European Union. In Murray and Rich, eds., 93–108.

Innis, H.A. 1930. *The fur trade in Canada: An introduction to Canadian economic history.* New Haven: Yale University Press.

Johnson, D. 2006. *Thinking government: Public sector management in Canada.* 2nd ed. Toronto: Broadview.

Joly, M. 2007. *Le mythe Jean Monnet: Contribution à une sociologie historique de la construction européenne.* Paris: CNRS.

Kallmann, H., G. Potvin, and K. Winters. 1992. *Encyclopedia of music in Canada.* Toronto: University of Toronto Press.

Kelly, C. Brian, and Ingrid Smyer-Kelly. 2008. *Best little stories from the life and times of Winston Churchill.* Nashville, TN: Cumberland House.

Kingwell, M., and C. Moore. 1999. *Canada: Our century.* Toronto: Doubleday Canada.

Kissinger, H. 1982. *Years of upheaval.* Boston: Little, Brown.

Laffan, B. 1998. The European Union: A distinctive model of Europeanization. *Journal of European Public Policy* 5 (2): 235–53.

Lebovics, H. 1992. *True France: The wars over cultural identity.* Ithaca: Cornell University Press.

March, J.G., and H. Simon. 1993. *Organizations.* 2nd ed. Cambridge, UK: Blackwell.

Marjolin, R. 1991. What type of Europe? In Brinkley and Hackett, 163–83.

Mayne, R. 1962. *The community of Europe: Past, present and future.* New York: Norton.

McInnis, E. 1969. *Canada: A political and social history.* Toronto: Holt, Rinehart and Winston of Canada.

Monnet, J. 1955. *Les États-Unis d'Europe ont commencé: la Communauté européenne du charbon et de l'acier, discours et allocutions, 1952–1954.* Paris: Robert Laffont.

– 1961. Western unity: The cornerstone of world peace. *Réalités Monthly Magazine,* December, 133.

– 1976. *Memoires.* Paris: Fayard.

– 1978. *Memoirs.* Garden City: Doubleday.

Murray, P., and P. Rich. 1996. Introduction. In Murray and Rich, eds., 1–20.

– eds. 1996. *Visions of European unity.* Boulder: Westview.

Nathan, R.R. 1991. An unsung hero of World War II. In Brinkley and Hackett, 67–85.

Navari, C. 1996. Functionalism and federalism: Alternative visions of European unity. In Murray and Rich, eds., 63–91.

Newman, P.C. 1991. *Merchant princes: Company of adventurers.* Toronto: Viking.

Newsweek. 1950. Coal, steel, and the Monnet spark plug. 19 June.

New York Times. 1907. Richard Mansfield back: Actor arrives in Montreal, not improved in health. 27 July.

Nowlan, A. 1975. *Campobello: The outer island.* Toronto: Clarke, Irwin.

Olsen, J.P. 1997. Institutional design in democratic contexts. *Journal of Political Philosophy* 5 (3): 203–29.

– 2007. *Europe in search of political order: An institutional perspective on unity/diversity, citizens/their helpers, democratic design/historical drift, and the co-existence of orders.* New York: Oxford University Press.

Pentland, C. 1981. Political theories of European integration: Between science and ideology. In *The European communities in action,* ed. D. Lasok and P. Soldatos, 545–69. Brussels: Bruylant.

Pierson, P. 2004. *Politics in time: History, institutions, and social analysis.* Princeton: Princeton University Press.

Popham, R.E., and W. Schmidt. 1958. *Statistics of alcohol use and alcoholism in Canada 1871–1956.* Toronto: University of Toronto Press.

Prestwich, P.E. 1979. Temperance in France: The curious case of absinth. *Historical Reflections* 6 (2): 301–19.

Rawlinson, G. 1859. *The history of Herodotus.* New York: Appleton.

Redfield, J. 1985. Herodotus the tourist. *Classical Philology* 80 (2): 97.

Rieben, H., C. Camperio-Tixier, and F. Nicod. 2004. *A L'Écoute de Jean Monnet.* Lausanne: Fondation Jean Monnet pour l'Europe.

Roger, P. 2005. *The American enemy: The history of French anti-Americanism.* Chicago: University of Chicago Press.

Rohmer, R. 1978. *E.P. Taylor: The biography of Edward Plunket Taylor.* Toronto: McClelland and Stewart.

Rostow, W.W. 1994. Jean Monnet: The innovator as diplomat. In *The diplomats 1939–1979*, ed. G.A. Craig and F.L. Loewenheim, 257–88. Princeton, NJ: Princeton University Press.

Roussel, E. 1996. *Jean Monnet*. Paris: Fayard.

Rumbelow, D. 1988. *The complete Jack the Ripper*. Harmondsworth, UK: Penguin.

Russell, P.H., R. Knopff, and T. Morton. 1989. *Federalism and the Charter: Leading constitutional decisions*. Ottawa: Carleton University Press.

Rutherford, I. 2000. Theoria and darśan: Pilgrimage and vision in Greece and India. *Classical Quarterly* 50 (1): 133–46.

Ryback, T.W. 1996. Dateline Sudetenland: Hostages to history. *Foreign Policy* (105): 162–78.

Schooling, W. 1920. *The governor and company of adventurers of England trading into Hudson's Bay during two hundred and fifty years, 1670–1920*. London: Hudson's Bay Company.

Skogstad, G. 2008. *Internationalization and Canadian agriculture: Policy and governing paradigms*. Toronto: University of Toronto Press.

Smart, R.G., and A.C. Ogborne. 1996. *Northern spirits: A social history of alcohol in Canada*. Toronto: Addiction Research Foundation.

Smiley, D.V. 1978. *The Rowell/Sirois Report / Book 1*. Ottawa: Macmillan Canada.

Taylor, F.W. 1911. *The principles of scientific management*. New York: Harper.

Thompson, N. 1996. *Herodotus and the origin of the political community*. New Haven: Yale University Press.

Time. 1961. Europe: Then will it live. 6 October.

– 2006. 60 years of heroes. 13 November.

Tocqueville, A. de. 2000. *Democracy in America*. Chicago: University of Chicago Press.

Ugland, T. 2003. A case of strange bedfellows in the EU: An institutional perspective on the French-Swedish cooperation on alcohol control. *Scandinavian Political Studies* 26 (3): 269–86.

– 2009. Designer Europeanization: Lessons from Jean Monnet. *European Legacy* 14 (1): 149–61.

Van Loon, R.J., and M.S. Whittington. 1987. *The Canadian political system: Environment, structure and process.* 4th ed. Toronto: McGraw-Hill Ryerson.

Verdun, A. 2009. *Twenty years of Jean Monnet projects in Canada.* Paper presented at the Jean Monnet Conference: 20 Years of Support for European Integration Studies, Brussels, 7–8 September.

Whyte, J.W. 1981. *Nuggets of gold for temperance campaigns.* Toronto: Coates.

Wolin, S.S. 2001. *Tocqueville between two worlds: The making of a political and theoretical life.* Princeton: Princeton University Press.

– 2004. *Politics and vision: Continuity and innovation in Western political thought.* Princeton: Princeton University Press.

Yergin, D., and J. Stanislaw. 1998. *The commanding heights: The battle between government and the marketplace that is remaking the modern world.* New York: Touchstone, Simon & Schuster.

Index

absinthe, 89n15
Action Committee for the United States of Europe, 70, 86
African Union (AU), 6, 94n55
Alberta, 22, 23, 34, 42, 76
Algeria, 86
Allan Line Steamship Company, 16, 19, 87n4
Anglo-French Coordinating Committee, 66–7
Archangel, 46
arsenal of democracy, 66
Asia Pacific Economic Cooperation (APEC), 6
Association of Southeast Asian Nations (ASEAN), 6
Atlantic Community, 15, 70
Australia, 25

Ball, George W., 28, 50, 55, 92n39
Barrault, M., 40
Bay Steam Ship Company, 47
Belgium, 13, 30, 46, 80

Bell, Alexander Graham, 89n11
Benon, Fernand, 44
Berthoin, Georges, 45, 91n32
Bidault, Georges, 27–9, 72
Blair and Co. Investment Bank, 54–5
Borden, Henry, 92n37
Bowie, Robert, 10
British Columbia, 22, 40, 89n12
British North America Act, 33
British Supply Council, 66–7, 85
Brook, Timothy, 35
Bulgaria, 10, 85
Bullitt, William C., 59–61, 65
Burbidge, Herbert, 40–1, 90n21
Burbidge, Richard, 40, 90n21

Calgary, 23, 42, 44
Campobello Island, 60, 93n43
Canada: century of, 21; Con-

federation of, 4, 27–8, 30,
33; Delegation of the European Commission to, 80;
Dominion of, 33–4; EU and,
79; federalism in, 25, 27;
immigration to, 22–3; referendum on prohibition in,
38; temperance movement
in, 37–8, 42, 91n28; Wheat
Boom in, 4, 21
Canadian Museum of Rail
Travel, 89n12
Canadian Pacific Railway
(CPR), 22–3, 42, 43, 87n4,
89n12
Canadian Scheme, 59–67
Chamberlain, Neville, 58
Charles I (king), 35
Charles II (king), 35
Charlottetown, 57
Chiang Kai-shek, 56
China, 11, 56, 85
Chinese Finance Development
Corporation, 56
Churchill, Winston, 66
Cognac: M. Jean Monnet of
Cognac (Davenport), 72, 79,
82; town of, 18, 85
Council of Europe, 26

Daladier, Édouard, 58–9, 64
Davenport, John, 78
Democracy in America (Tocqueville), 10
Drucker, Peter, 52–3
Drummond, Eric, 50
Dubois, Pierre, 5

Duchêne, François, 7, 8, 30,
47, 54, 55, 71, 74
Dulles, John Foster, 54–6, 58,
92n38
Dupuy, Pierre, 16
Dutch East India Company, 35

Egypt, 9, 11
Eisenhower, Dwight D., 54,
92n38
Encounter, 81, 94n61
European Coal and Steel Community (ECSC): establishment of, 13, 29–31, 77–8,
86, 94n55; federation of
the West and, 27; Franco-German reconciliation and,
28–30; ratification of, 30;
Schuman Plan and, 78, 86;
Treaty of Paris and, 6, 30, 86
European Commission, 79–80
European Community (EC), 7
European Movement, 26–7
European Union (EU), 6–7,
69

Finer, Samuel E., 5
Fontaine, François, 47–8, 75,
82
Ford, Henry, 53
Fordism, 53
Fort Selkirk, 39
Fort William, 40, 41
Fortune, 55, 72, 78
France: airplane purchases
during Second World
War, 59–60, 62, 65–8; anti-

Americanism in, 71; EU and, 71–2; North Atlantic Treaty Organization (NATO) and, 72; preparations for First World War and, 43–5

Franco-British Coordination Committee, 85

French National Liberation Committee, 67, 86

French Planning Commissariat, 75, 86

functionalism, 31

Geneva, 50

Germany: European Coal and Steel Community and, 13; 28–30; immigrants from, 23; Monnet and, 80; Second World War and, 61, 65

Golden Age of Travel, 16–17

Great Britain: First World War and, 44–5; Hudson's Bay Company and, 35; Monnet and, 27, 66, 81; Second World War and, 65–6

Greece, 11

Guinea, Republic of, 80

Halifax, 34

Hallstein, Walter, 76

Harper, Stephen, 79

Hennessy Cognac, 18, 40, 88n6

Henry, Robert Alexander Cecil (R.A.C.), 92n37

Herodotus, 9

Heyerdahl, Thor, 94n56

High Authority of the ECSC, 29, 30, 45, 86

Hitler, Adolf, 6, 58–9, 61, 65

Hong Kong, 57

Houjarray, 7, 86, 94n54, 94n56

Howe, Clarence Decatur (C.D.), 54, 66, 92n37

Hudson Bay, 36

Hudson's Bay Company: Canadian headquarters in Winnipeg of, 36, 39, 81, 90n19; early history of, 14, 21, 35–6; fur trade of, 30, 36; J.G. Monnet & Co. Cognac and, 14, 32, 40–2, 89n10, 90n20; London headquarters of, 36, 39, 40, 41, 44; as French government's purchasing agent during First World War, 15, 46–9

Ingrams, Frank, 46

institutionalism, 12–13

internationalization, 6

Italy, 13, 30, 85n4

Jackson, Jesse, 69, 73

Jean Monnet Action initiative, 79

Jean Monnet Association, 7, 87n1, 91n32

Jean Monnet European Year, 7

J.G. Monnet & Co. Cognac: establishment of, 18; financial difficulties of, 43, 47; Hudson's Bay contract of, 14, 32, 40–2, 89n10, 90n20;

international markets for, 17–18, 20; sale of, 18
Johnson, David, 76–7
Johnson, Lyndon B., 89n13, 92n39

Kennedy, John F., 29, 89n13, 92n39
Keynes, John Maynard, 67
Kindersley, Robert, 39, 46, 49, 55, 90n17
Kindersley, Saskatchewan, 90n17
Kissinger, Henry, 73
Kon-Tiki, 94n56
Kreuger, Ivar, 55–6
Kreuger & Toll, 55

Labrador, 36
Laurier, Wilfrid, 21, 38
Lazard Brothers, 55
League of Nations, 26, 50, 54, 58, 85
Lebovics, Herman, 24
Lend-Lease, 93n51
Lindbergh, Anne Morrow, 93n50
Lindbergh, Charles, 64–5, 93n50
la liqueur des dieux (Hugo), 18
Liverpool, 17, 19, 46, 87n4
Lorraine, 29
Luftwaffe, 59, 65
Luxembourg, 13, 30, 80

Manitoba, 22, 42, 81
Mansfield, Richard, 17, 87–8n5

March, James G., 92n36
Marconi, Guglielmo, 89n11
Marjolin, Robert, 73
Marne, Battle of the, 45
Marshall Plan, 27
Martell Cognac, 18, 40
McInnis, Edgar, 33–4, 37
Monaco, 80
Monnet, Gaston, 19, 88n7
Monnet, Henriette, 88n7
Monnet, Jean
    Anglo-French Coordinating Committee and, 66
    Anglo-French Purchasing Board and, 66
    apprenticeship in London of, 19
    Atlantic Community initiative of, 15, 70
    balance sheet of, 65, 93n52
    Canada as inspirational model for, 8, 10, 11, 20, 51, 61, 69–83
    Canadian legacy of, 78–83
    creativity of, 45, 51, 61, 74
    education of, 5, 9, 18, 19, 27
    English skills of, 45
    family of, 18–19, 88n7
    first long voyage of, 17, 19
    First World War and, 15, 26, 44, 46–50, 54, 56, 81
    French airplane purchases and, 59–60, 62, 65–8
    French Civil Supplies Service and, 45–6, 85
    full name of, 85
    health problems of, 43–4

as honorary citizen of Europe, 7, 80, 86
international finance and, 54–8
as leader, 7, 37, 50, 54, 69–70, 77–8
League of Nations and, 26, 50, 54, 58, 85
memoirs of, 8, 47–8, 82, 86
method of, 30–1, 45, 70
Monnet, Murnane & Co. and, 56–7, 85
'old world' and 'new world' of, 3, 15, 20, 24–5, 28, 37, 40, 69–75
as optimist, 28, 37, 75
patience of, 37, 39, 49–50
personal economy of, 55
relationship with the United States of, 8, 68, 70–2, 85
Second World War and, 52–68
tenacity of, 39, 50
theory of supranational unity of, 8, 10, 13, 20, 25–32, 73, 78
walking habits of, 32
Monnet, Jean-Gabriel, 18, 59, 88n7, 90n22, 90n24
Monnet, Maria Demelle, 43, 88n7, 91n30
Monnet, Marianne, 71
Monnet, Marie Louise, 88n7
Monnet, Silvia de Bondini, 85
Monnet, Murnane & Co., 56–7, 85
Montreal, 19, 39, 46, 64, 87n4

Montreal Ocean Steamship Company, 87n4
Morgenthau, Jr, Henry, 61–2, 64
Morrow, Dwight, 78, 93n50
Morton, Anne, 81, 94n61
Munich Agreement, 58
Murnane, George, 56–8, 85
Mussolini, Benito, 58

Nathan, Robert R., 66
nationalism, 7, 11, 24, 28, 69, 73
natural resources and political integration, 29–30
Netherlands, 13, 30
Neutrality Act, 61–5
New Brunswick, 60, 88n6
New Deal, 62
Newman, Peter C., 36
Newsweek, 6
New York, 46
North American Free Trade Agreement (NAFTA), 6
North Atlantic Treaty Organization (NATO), 72
Northwest Territories, 34
Nova Scotia, 89n11
Nunavut, 36

Ontario, 40, 44
Organization for European Economic Co-operation (OEEC), 27

Pantheon, 72, 86
Paris Peace Conference, 54

Pierson, Paul, 12, 77
placing politics in time, 11–14
Poland, 11, 50, 54, 65, 85
Port Arthur, 44
Portugal, 80
Prince Edward Island, 38, 57
Prince Edward Island Joint
    Stock Company Act, 57
*Principles of Scientific Manage-
    ment* (Taylor), 53
Purvis, Arthur, 66, 94n53

Quebec: city of, 16, 17, 19, 20;
    province of, 38, 87n4
Quebec Bridge, 20

Red River, 36
regional integration, 6–7,
    94n55
Rémy Martin Cognac, 18
Rocky Mountains, 32, 36
Romania, 11, 54
Roosevelt, Eleanor, 68
Roosevelt, Franklin Delano:
    Canada and, 59–60, 93n43;
    Monnet and, 59–62, 65–8,
    94n54
Roosevelt, Jr, Franklin Delano,
    60
Rostow, Walt W., 25, 89n13
Royal Alexandra Hotel, 89n12
Roussel, Éric, 7
Rumbelow, Daniel, 87n5
Rumsfeld, Donald, 71
Rupert of the Rhine (prince),
    35
Rupert's Land, 35–6

Russia, 11, 46, 85, 88n6

Saint John, 87n4
Sale, Charles, 39, 46, 48, 90n17
Sarkozy, Nicolas, 72, 79
Saskatchewan, 22, 23, 34, 42,
    90n17
Scandinavia, 23, 88n6
Scharlachberg, 18
Schuman, Robert: background
    of, 29; Monnet's appeals to,
    27, 29; Schuman Plan press
    conference of, 29
Scott, Gordon, 92n37
Sifton, Clifford, 21
Simon, Herbert A., 92n36
Soldatos, Panayotis, 80
Southern Common Market
    (MERCOSUR), 6
Soviet Union, 28
Spain, 80
Staden, Berndt von, 76
St Lawrence River, 20, 34
*Strange Case of Dr Jekyll and Mr
    Hyde* (Stevenson), and Jack
    the Ripper, 87–8n5
Superior, Lake, 40
Sweden, 11, 55, 85
Switzerland, 32

Taylor, Edward Plunket (E.P.),
    92n37
Taylor, Frederick W., 52–3,
    92n36
theoria, 9, 11, 53, 67, 70, 71,
    81
Time, 7, 72

Tocqueville, Alexis de, 10–11, 24–5
Transamerica Corporation, 55
travelling and political theory, 9–11, 24, 75
Trieste, 87n4
True France (Lebovics), 24

United States: as 'arsenal of democracy,' 59–67; Atlantic Community and, 70–1; Europe and, 71; Monnet and, 8, 15, 72, 85; Prohibition in, 51
United Vineyard Proprietors Company (UVPC), 18, 41
Upper Silesia, 50

Vancouver, 39
Vancouver Island, 40

Verdun, Amy, 80
Victory Program, 67, 82
Virginian, 16–17, 19, 87n4
Viviani, René, 44–5

Whyte, David A., 91n28
Whyte, John M., 42–1, 91n28
Winnipeg: boom time in, 22–3; Hudson's Bay Company in, 36, 39, 81, 90n19; Monnet and, 3–4, 40, 43, 52, 81; Royal Alexandra Hotel in, 23, 89n12
Winnipeg General Hospital, 43–4
Wolin, Sheldon S., 9–11, 25, 32

Yukon, 39

European Union Studies

Catherine Gegout, *European Foreign and Security Policy: States, Power, Institutions, and American Hegemony*

Frédéric Mérand, Martial Foucault, and Bastien Irondelle, eds., *European Security since the Fall of the Berlin Wall*

Trygve Ugland, *Jean Monnet and Canada: Early Travels and the Idea of European Unity*